THE LAST PATROL

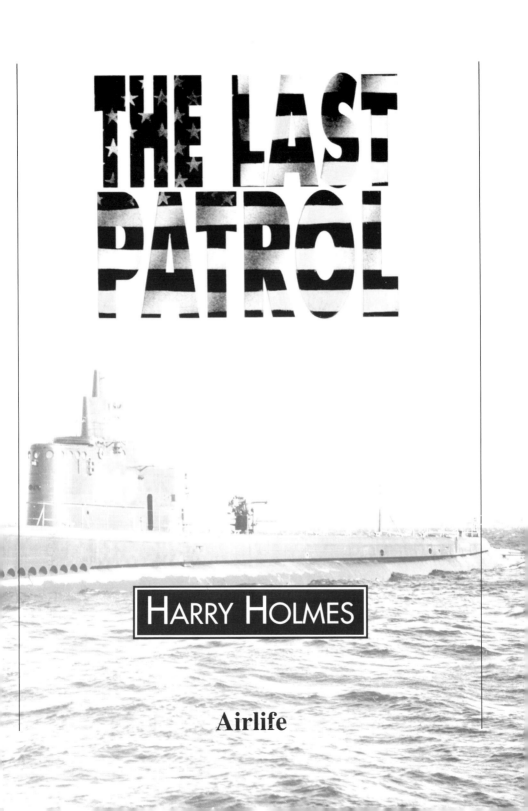

THE LAST PATROL

HARRY HOLMES

Airlife

Dedication

*To all the gallant submariners who lie forever
in the deep oceans of the world . . .*

Copyright © 1994 by Harry Holmes

First published in the UK in 1994
by Airlife Publishing Ltd

British Cataloguing in Publication Data
   A catalogue record for this book
   is available from the British Library

ISBN 1 85310 414 0

Printed in England by Livesey Ltd., Shrewsbury.

Airlife Publishing Ltd.

101 Longden Road, Shrewsbury SY3 9EB, England

Contents

Acknowledgements

I would like to express my warmest appreciation for the assistance I have received during the preparation of this book.

Firstly, for the encouragement received from Admiral Bernard A. Clarey, USN (Ret), wartime commander of the famed USS *Pintado* and who was the first executive officer of the USS *Amberjack*, which features in this work. Encouragement also came from Captain Edward L. Beach, USN (Ret), famous submariner and author of many books on the subject including *Run Silent, Run Deep*. Captain Beach served as executive officer of the USS *Trigger*, which is also described in this book.

Thanks are also due for photographic assistance, especially Mr Russell D. Egnor, Director of the United States Navy Department's News Photo Division. Assistance also came from the Pacific Fleet Memorial Association and the USS *Bowfin* Submarine Museum at Pearl Harbor; the US Naval Institute; the National Archives; the *Nautilus* Memorial Submarine Force Library & Museum and also the Manitowoc Maritime Museum. Because of the nature of submarine operations all pictures used in the books are official photographs.

I would also like to thank Mr Stan Nicholls, an official of the USS *Bowfin* Museum and who completed a number of war patrols in the USS *Pompon*, for his encouragement and unforgettable tour of the Submarine Base at Pearl Harbor.

Last, but by no means least, I would like to thank Fiona Mann for typing the manuscript and for the interest and encouragement she showed while she was doing so.

US Submarine Operations Against Japan

United States submarine operations were one of the most important features in the defeat of the Japanese with their offensive accounting for almost two-thirds of the total losses of the Japanese merchant marine and one-third of the sinkings of the Imperial Japanese Navy.

When the US Pacific Fleet was badly mauled by the Japanese attack on Pearl Harbor on 7 December 1941, it fell to the submarines to carry the war to the enemy. At that time there were fifty-one US submarines in the Pacific including twelve of the old 'S' Class.

Operating deep within Japanese-controlled waters their campaign of attrition began almost immediately and although a number of early attacks were reported, the first confirmed sinking was on 16 December when the USS *Swordfish* (SS-193) torpedoed the *Atsutasan Maru*, a 8,663-ton freighter, off Hainan Island in the South China Sea. It was to be the first of many and a dubious distinction.

Japan as an island nation depended on oil, rubber, coal and rice from its conquests and it was a tactical mistake that many of their merchant ships sailed unescorted and were duly despatched by patrolling submarines. It was not until late in 1943 that anti-submarine tactics began to emerge and it was also unfortunate for the submarine force that earlier in the war a group of United States politicians had visited Pacific Submarine Headquarters at Pearl Harbor and, upon returning to the USA, reported to the media that Japanese depth-charges were not large enough and were not set deep enough to harm US submarines. Needless to say, this information was gratefully received by the Japanese and changes were quickly incorporated.

The destruction of the Japanese merchant fleet rose from 134 vessels totalling 580,390 tons in 1942 to 284 ships for 1,341,986 tons in 1943. As the number of submarines increased and torpedoes improved, the 1944 total reached 2,387,780 tons from 492 merchant ships and these figures did not include the hundreds of vessels of less than 1,000 tons.

Many of these smaller ships were sunk by gunfire in the late war period. In 1945 with targets becoming scarce US submarines sent 132 merchant ships to the bottom for a total loss of 469,872 tons. Nearly five million tons of Japan's merchant marine were sunk including 104 of their vitally-needed tankers.

The Imperial Japanese Navy also suffered greatly at the hands of the submarine force with a battleship, nine aircraft-carriers, twelve cruisers, forty-three destroyers and twenty-three submarines paying the ultimate price. Nearly 200 smaller vessels, including escort craft, should be added to that total.

The final tonnage total would have been much greater, but for the poor performance of American torpedoes which had defects in the depth-control system and the firing mechanism. Many US submarine commanders were driven to despair when solid hits resulted in no explosions or when the torpedo exploded prematurely thereby giving away the boat's presence, sometimes subjecting it to a heavy depth-charging if the target was escorted. It was not until September 1943 that the problems were finally solved and the submarines could put to sea with reliable torpedoes. The total was also reduced at the war's end by the US Joint Army-Navy Assessment Committee (JANAC) who dismissed many claims of Japanese ship sinkings because the Japanese had poorly-kept records and unexplained omissions in reports. Whether this was for security or morale reasons it will never be known, but the final scores of many submarines were drastically reduced even though vessels had been seen to go down.

Although the sinking of Japanese shipping was the primary objective of United States submarines, many special missions were undertaken with great effect. Missions performed by submarines included evacuations, supply, mine laying, reconnaissance and lifeguard duties. In the early days of the war, submarines were called upon to rescue personnel from Bataan and Corregidor and keep the Philippine resistance fighters well supplied with arms and ammunition.

Reconnaissance tasks continued throughout the war with information supplied for the first bombing raid on Japan when sixteen B-25 medium bombers were launched from the carrier USS *Hornet* (CV-8), to the vital information prior to the Battle for Leyte Gulf; these being just two outstanding examples of the reconnaissance role played by submarines.

As the large carrier task forces and the B-29 raids on the Japanese mainland gathered momentum, US submarines carried out some daring rescues of flyers forced down into the sea. A total of 504 aviators were picked up by submarines including a certain Lt George Bush, a future President of the United States, who was rescued from his dinghy by the USS *Finback* (SS-230) after being shot down.

Although the wolf-pack system was operated to some degree later in the war, American submarines usually operated alone, far from base and deep into the enemy zone where friendly surface ships and aircraft could not operate.

Of the fifty-two submarines lost through all causes, thirty-seven were lost with all hands, yet there was no shortage of volunteers for submarine duty and with an excellent build programme the number of vessels far exceeded the pre-Pearl Harbor strength by the war's end.

No report of the United States submarines' contribution to the final victory in the Pacific could be complete without some account of those that did not return. This is their story.

Sealion's launching was at Groton on 25 May 1939.

US Submarines Lost in World War II
(Chronological order)

The completed *Sealion* on her sea trials.

USS *Sealion* (SS-195)

The *Sealion* was launched by Mrs Claude C. Block on 25 May 1939 at the Electric Boat Company, Groton, Connecticut. After completion the boat was commissioned on 27 November 1939.

Under the command of Lt J. K. Morrison, Jr, *Sealion* completed her shakedown cruise and joined the Asiatic Fleet arriving at Cavite in the Philippines in August 1940. After taking part in a number of exercises, *Sealion* was undergoing overhaul in the Cavite Navy Yard when Pearl Harbor was attacked. On 10 December 1941 Cavite came under attack from Japanese Mitsubishi Navy Attack Bombers based in Formosa and *Sealion*, then commanded by Lt-Cmdr Richard G. Voge, was struck by two bombs during the raid. The first hit the rear of the conning tower, while the second bomb penetrated the pressure hull and exploded in the after engine room killing the four men working in there.

The *Sealion's* stern sank to the bottom as the boat started to flood and she settled with half of her hull underwater and with a ten-degree list to starboard. Her sister ship USS *Seadragon* (SS-194), which was moored alongside, received heavy structural damage from bomb fragments. The minesweeper USS *Pidgeon* (ASR-6) was able to tow *Seadragon* out to the clear channel where she then got under way after temporary repairs.

The heavy bombing of the Navy Yard made the extensive repairs required by *Sealion* totally impossible and she was ordered to be destroyed to prevent capture and possible use by the Japanese. With all useful equipment salvaged three depth-charges were placed aboard and these were detonated on Christmas Day 1941.

In 1945, as US forces liberated the Philippines, Navy personnel were amazed to find the wreck of the *Sealion* still in place. Who knows what havoc she could have caused to the Japanese if those two bombs had missed on that fateful December day.

All that remained of *Sealion* after the Japanese air attack on Cavite Navy Yard in the Philippines, 10 December 1941.

USS *S-36* (SS-141)

S-36 was one of the twelve old 'Sugar' boats operating in the Pacific on 7 December 1941. She was launched on 3 June 1919 at Bethlehem Shipbuilding Company of San Francisco, but as World War I had ended, work slowed and S-36 was not commissioned until 4 April 1923.

At the time of the Japanese attack on Pearl Harbor the *S-36* was on patrol off Luzon and this continued until 20 December when she was forced to put into Mariveles on the Bataan peninsula after a number of mechanical failures.

After repairs had been completed and the boat resupplied, the *S-36* departed for her second patrol on 30 December with orders to patrol the Verde Island Passage. New Year's Day 1942 brought the submarine an unexpected bonus when her commander, Lt John R. McKnight, sighted a Japanese cargo ship of approximately 5,000 tons moored in the harbour at Calapan, Mindoro. After a quick look around for hostile warships, Lt McKnight fired one torpedo which hit solidly and he was amazed to see the vessel sink almost immediately.

The *S-36*, encouraged by this success, went looking for other targets out into the Sulu Sea, but on the morning of 15 January while running on the surface she was sighted by a Japanese destroyer. As the boat prepared to dive there was an oil lubrication failure in the starboard engine and McKnight had to take her down on one engine. He quickly prepared to fire at the warship, but the lost engine had slowed the dive and the advantage was with the destroyer.

The Japanese dropped seven depth-charges with the *S-36* immediately losing control over the bow planes; a gyro compass failed and also numerous electrical faults occurred. At slow speed, with control and trim troublesome, the submarine tried to escape the attacker, but it was difficult and as things looked desperate, the commander gave the order to issue escape equipment and life-jackets. However, two hours after the initial attack, control was restored and McKnight skilfully guided *S-36* away from the still searching destroyer.

Early in the morning of 16 January the starboard engine's lubrication problem returned and as dawn approached she submerged as Japanese sea and air activity in the Celebes area was on the increase. At midday fire broke out in the motor, but it was quickly extinguished. Then followed a series of failures and other

The *S-36* is seen here soon after completion.

problems and it was the 18th before things were running smoothly once more.

On 20 January she was proceeding through the Makassar Strait *en route* to Surabaya, Java, when at 0404 hrs she ran aground on a reef at Taka Baking. This was, without doubt, through the use of inadequate charts, but they were the only ones available at the time. The crew fought hard to save the *S-36*, but chlorine gas from the flooded forward battery room and rough seas combined to make it an impossible task. A distress call was sent out and a Dutch ship, the *Attla*, was despatched to aid the stricken submarine. The boat was flooded further to prevent capture and forty-seven crew members were safely taken off at 1330 hrs on 21 January 1942.

The crew of the *S-36* eventually reached Surabaya on the steamer SS *Siberote* and were later reassigned, with Lt McKnight later commanding the USS *Porpoise* (SS-172).

The *S-36* received one battle star for her short active service life in which she deprived the Japanese of one valuable freighter.

USS *S-26* (SS-131)

The *S-26* was launched by the Bethlehem Shipbuilding Company of Quincy, Massachusetts on 22 August 1922 and commissioned on 15 October 1923.

She served on many peacetime cruises, with the start of World War II seeing her based at New London, Connecticut. Three days after the Japanese attack she sailed from her base arriving at Coco Solo in the Canal Zone on 19 December 1941.

On January 1942 the *S-26* left Balboa on her second war patrol in the Gulf of Panama. Other 'Sugar' boats accompanied her including the *S-21*, *S-29* and *S-44* with the submarines being escorted by the patrol craft *PC-460*.

Bethlehem Shipbuilding launched the *S-26* into the Fore River.

At 2210 hrs the *PC-460* flashed a message by signal lamp to the submarines cruising on the surface confirming that she was about to leave the group. Apparently, *S-21* was the only boat to receive the message and at 2223 hrs after turning to leave the formation the escort vessel collided in the darkness with *S-26* hitting the starboard side of the torpedo room. The submarine sank immediately taking forty-six crew members down with her. The only survivors were the commanding officer Lt-Cmdr Earl C. Hawk, the Executive Officer Robert E. M. Ward and one enlisted man who were all on the bridge at the time. Another enlisted man on the bridge went down with the boat. Three other crew members survived as they were in the base hospital at the time of the *S-26's* departure. Salvage operations were started almost immediately but the *S-26* had sunk too deep and rescue was impossible.

The surviving officers went on to successful commands; Hawk in USS *Pompon* (SS-267) and Ward in the USS *Sailfish* (SS-192) with his score including the 20,000-ton aircraft-carrier *Chuyo*.

A between-the-wars shot of the *S-26* and her crew at Pearl Harbor.

USS *Shark* (SS-174)

The 21 May 1935 saw the launch of *Shark* at the Electric Boat Company's yard at Groton, Connecticut. The launching ceremony was carried out by Miss Ruth Ellen Lonergan. The boat was commissioned on 25 January 1936 under the command of Lt C. J. Carter.

A bow view of *Shark* as she was being prepared for launching.

On 7 December 1941 she was part of the Asiatic Fleet and two days later she departed from Manila just in time to escape the heavy bombing which took place the following day.

Shark, under the command of Lt-Cmdr Lewis Shane Jr, was assigned to Tayabas Bay for her first war patrol. On the 19th she was ordered to return to Manila in order to evacuate Admiral Thomas C. Hart, Commander-in-Chief of the US Asiatic Fleet and his staff, to Surabaya, Java. This completed, *Shark* returned to her patrol and on 6 January 1942 a Japanese submarine fired a torpedo which missed her by a matter of feet. After patrolling the Ambon Island area to guard against the expected invasion, she was ordered to the Molucca Passage. On 2 February *Shark* reported to her base in Surabaya that she had been depth-charged by a Japanese destroyer, later identified as the IJN *Amatsukaze*, ten miles off Tifore Island. The report also stated that she made an unsuccessful torpedo attack on the destroyer.

On 7 February she reported that she had sighted a cargo ship which was high out of the water and presumably empty and she was shadowing. On the 8th *Shark* was instructed to Makassar Strait via the north coast of Celebes. No further messages were received from her and on 7 March 1942 *Shark* was reported overdue and presumed lost.

Shark could have been lost through operational causes, as Japanese records show that there were a number of attacks on unidentified submarines in that area and about that time. The most likely of these was on 11 February. The destroyer IJN *Yamakaze* sighted a submarine on the surface at 0137 hrs and opened fire with her main armament. Soon the submarine sank from sight and voices were heard in the water; however, the Japanese made no attempt to pick up any survivors, and *Shark* and her fifty-eight crew members disappeared forever.

Carrying her original number P-3, *Shark* departs past 'Battleship Row', Pearl Harbor, in this pre-war photograph.

USS *Perch* (SS-176)

Perch was launched 9 May 1936 by Mrs Thomas Withers at the Electric Boat Company, Groton, Connecticut. The first Commanding Officer was Lt-Cmdr G. C. Crawford when the submarine was commissioned on 19 November 1936.

On 1 December 1941 *Perch*, under the command of Lt-Cmdr David A. Hurt and part of the Asiatic Fleet, escorted two transports carrying the 4th Marine Division from China to the Philippines. At the time of the attack on Pearl Harbor she was in Cavite Navy Yard, but was ordered out that night to patrol in the South China Sea.

Amazingly, targets were scarce and it was not until Christmas

Launching day for *Perch*.

Perch wearing the number P-5 is seen in this shot dated 17 June 1937.

night that *Perch* made her first attack when she sighted a fast convoy. Hurt fired four torpedoes at a large freighter, but all missed. On 27 December *Perch* tried once more and this time two torpedoes found their mark with Hurt reporting the vessel as sunk. This ship was later claimed to be the 7,190-ton *Nojima Maru* and although this freighter was never heard of again, *Perch* was never credited with its sinking because the arrival of enemy escorts prevented Hurt from confirming the loss.

Perch received orders to proceed to Port Darwin, Australia, for some minor repairs and resupply. She departed from the base on 3 February 1942 for her second patrol with the submarine scouting the Java Sea and up into the Makassar Strait. Off the coast of Celebes on 25 February *Perch* made a night surface attack on a small convoy, but the enemy gunners were accurate, slamming a shell into her conning tower after a number of near misses. The hit badly damaged the bridge and antenna trunk putting the radio out of action, causing her to withdraw quickly from the fight.

Running repairs were carried out and a message was sent to Headquarters telling them that radio reception was, hopefully, possible but it was thought that her transmissions could be uncertain. On the night of 1 March *Perch* was off the coast near Surabaya to attack a Japanese force landing soldiers on Java itself.

She was sighted by two Japanese destroyers, the IJN *Amatsukaze* and the *Hatsukaze* and Hurt 'pulled the plug' taking *Perch* down into deep water, but once again charts proved to be inaccurate and she bottomed at approximately 140 feet burying her bow into the sea-bed. She was then subjected to an intensive depth-charging causing a great amount of damage, but convinced that the submarine had been destroyed, the enemy warships departed from the scene. After repairs *Perch* surfaced in the early morning of the 2nd only to be forced down and subjected to another heavy depth-charge attack resulting in more damage. Loss of air and oil from *Perch* obviously once again convinced the Japanese that she had been destroyed and the vessels gave up the attack.

Perch surfaced at 2100 hrs after much repair work and Hurt decided to head for the nearest friendly port. Barely making five knots on one engine and still leaking badly, the damage repair crews worked hard and the problems eased. Feeling vulnerable on the surface, Hurt decided on a trial dive in the early hours of 3 March but this was almost fatal as water poured in again and the boat had to struggle to the surface.

The main difficulty appeared to be a sprung hatch in the conning tower and a repair party was sent to solve the problem. As work was in progress Japanese warships were sighted and shells from the destroyers *Sazanami* and *Ushio* began to splash around *Perch*.

Unable to fight or run Lt-Cmdr Hurt decided that the only course of action was to scuttle the submarine to prevent further shelling and possible death to crew members or, perhaps, her capture. The order to abandon ship was given and with all vents and hatches open, *Perch* began her last dive.

The crew of sixty-two was picked up by the Japanese and received rough treatment at the hands of their captors. Nine were to die in prisoner-of-war camps but fifty-three, including the commanding officer, were released at the war's end and the full story of *Perch's* final battle became known.

The *S-27* seen in the late 1920s.

USS *S-27* (SS-132)

S-27 was launched 18 October 1922 at the Quincy Plant of the Bethlehem Shipbuilding Company and was commissioned on 22 January 1924 with her first commanding officer being Lt Ted Waldschmidt.

After taking part in many fleet exercises and training missions in the years between the wars, *S-27* was at Mare Island Navy Yard, California, for overhaul when the United States entered World War II.

With the overhaul completed she was assigned to the sound school at San Diego and operated on a number of training missions but on 20 May 1942 *S-27*, under the command of Lt Herbert L. Jukes, proceeded to Dutch Harbor to join the submarine force patrolling the Aleutian Islands.

On 18 June, *S-27* was on the reconnaissance in the Amchitka Island area with the long Arctic daylight hours meaning that only a short period of darkness was available each day to surface and charge batteries. With the mission completed, Jukes brought the submarine to the surface in hazy conditions, a regular feature of the poor weather which prevailed in that area, and proceeded with the battery charge. With visibility almost nil it went unnoticed that the current was forcing the submarine shorewards and the *S-27* grounded on a reef of solid rock 400 yards off the coast at St Makarius Point at 0043 hrs on the 19th.

The boat was firmly wedged and all through the short night the crew worked hard to free her but it was an impossible task and at 1550 hrs with heavy seas breaking over her Lt Jukes ordered the *S-27* to be abandoned.

The forty-nine-man crew all reached shore safely using only one rubber boat in relay fashion and were saddened to see the submarine being slowly broken up by the pounding waves. They found an abandoned village and made camp there until they were spotted by a searching PBY flying-boat. Later that day they were rescued by this and other aircraft.

The crew were later reassigned throughout the submarine force and Lt, later Lt-Cmdr Jukes destroyed a number of Japanese vessels as commander of the Fleet Submarine USS *Kingfish* (SS-234).

Grunion at New London on 20 March 1942 during the build-up to her commissioning.

The Japanese patrol boat *Ch.25* sunk by *Grunion* off Kiska, 15 July 1942.

USS *Grunion* (SS-216)

Grunion was launched by Mrs Stamford C. Hooper, wife of Rear Admiral Hooper, on 22 December 1941 at the Electric Boat Company's construction yard at Groton, Connecticut. She was placed under the command of Lt-Cmdr Mannert L. Abele and commissioned 11 April 1942.

After a shakedown cruise *Grunion* was assigned to the Pacific and departed New London on 24 May. On the 28th she sighted a lifeboat carrying sixteen seamen and upon stopping to rescue them she discovered that they were American from the 2,822-ton steamer *Jack** which had been torpedoed that morning. She spent the rest of the daylight hours searching for any remaining survivors, but without success. The survivors were landed at Coco Solo on 3 June and *Grunion* continued on to Pearl Harbor arriving on the 20th.

She left Pearl Harbor on 30 June and after calling at Midway Island to top up her fuel tanks, the submarine headed north to the Aleutians for her first war patrol. Grunion was ordered to patrol north of Kiska and on 15 July she reported that she had been attacked by an enemy destroyer and that she had fired three torpedoes at the vessel, but they all missed.

Later that same day she reported that she had engaged three Japanese submarine chasers, sank two and badly damaged the third. After the war Japanese records confirmed that *Grunion* had indeed sunk the *Ch.25* and *Ch.27*.

On 19 July she joined other US submarines patrolling the approaches to Kiska Harbor and on the 28th reported an unsuccessful attack on enemy shipping and a subsequent depth charging.

Her last report on the 30th told of heavy anti-submarine activity in her patrol station and she was ordered to leave the area and proceed to Dutch Harbor. *Grunion* and her crew of seventy were never seen or heard of again.

The loss of *Grunion* will always remain a mystery, with the post-war examination of Japanese records failing to reveal the cause. A number of theories have been put forward, but all have been discounted in one way or another.

Grunion received one battle star for her short life and a United States destroyer, the USS *Mannert L. Abele* (DD-733) was named in honour of the submarine's commanding officer. Unfortunately, she too was lost when hit by two Kamikaze suicide aircraft off Okinawa on 12 April 1945.

* The *Jack* had been sunk by the German submarine *U-155* commanded by Lt Adolf Piening.

USS *S-39* (SS-144)

The *S-39*, built by the Bethlehem Shipbuilding Company in San Francisco was launched on 2 July 1919, but was not commissioned until more than four years later on 14 September 1923.

At the outbreak of hostilities in the Pacific the *S-39*, under the command of Lt James W. 'Red' Coe was on patrol off Luzon, but was immediately ordered to the San Bernardino Strait to attack Japanese minelayers known to be active in that area. The enemy minelaying activities were well escorted and on the 11th *S-39* was subjected to a long and heavy depth-charge attack. On the 13th she sighted a Japanese freighter of some 5,000 tons and after an unsuccessful attack, the escorts again appeared on the scene forcing Coe to abandon the attack. After no more sightings she returned to Manila arriving on the 21st.

The Christmas period was not a happy one in the Philippines and Coe was ordered to take the submarine to Surabaya, Java, where she arrived on 24 January 1942 with her transit being confirmed as the *S-39's* second war patrol. After a short resupply period she set out on her third war patrol with orders to operate in the Java and South China Seas. It was during that patrol that the boat was ordered on a special mission to rescue Rear-Admiral Spooner, RN, and a group of British refugees from the recently-captured garrison at Singapore. The party had sought refuge on the small island of Chebia in the South China Sea. The *S-39* reached the island on 27 February well before the arranged rendezvous time, but after two days of waiting with no apparent activity, Coe decided to lead a shore party to search for the British group. There was no shortage of volunteers and the submariners landed ready for any trouble that could come their way. However the search was unsuccessful as the island was completely deserted, but tracks in the sand suggested a small boat carrying soldiers had captured the refugees.

After that mission she returned to the Java Sea in search of targets and on 4 March 1942 the *S-39* made a submerged attack on the 6,500-ton tanker *Erimo* sending it to the bottom with three solid torpedo hits.

On 18 March she arrived in Fremantle, Australia, but five weeks later she reported to Brisbane as her new home base. She also had a new skipper, Lt Francis E. Brown and the *S-39* left Brisbane for her fourth war patrol on 10 May, but this was unsuccessful with no sightings of the Japanese.

Her fifth patrol was delayed twice by mechanical failures, then, as

S-39 seen in pre-war fleet exercises off the Californian coast.

the problems were cleared, her executive officer was rushed to hospital with pneumonia and a replacement had to be found. She finally departed on 10 August and after battling against heavy seas and high winds the *S-39* was supposed to be east of Rossel Island in the Louisiades on the 13th, but an error in navigation was discovered the hard way when the boat went onto a submerged reef to the south of the island at 0200 hrs on 14 August. Brown ordered the ballast tanks to be blown and everything possible done to lighten the submarine, but even with engines on back-emergency she would not move.

Heavy seas pounded the *S-39*, but the crew was fighting a lost cause and on the 16th the Australian minesweeper HMAS *Katoomba* arrived to evacuate the forty-four crew members. As the minesweeper left the scene the submarine was already breaking up with the relentless battering by the waves.

The *S-39* was awarded two battle stars for her service and her commander, Lt Brown, was later assigned to the *S-44* (SS-155) only to be lost in that boat. The *S-39's* previous wartime skipper, 'Red' Coe would be the successful commander of the USS *Skipjack* (SS-184) before losing his life in the USS *Cisco* (SS-290).

USS *Argonaut* (SS-166)

The largest submarine used by the United States Navy in World War II was the 385-feet long, 2,710-ton *Argonaut*. She was built by the Portsmouth Navy Yard, New Hampshire, and launched as the *V-4* on 10 November 1927. Commissioned on 2 April 1928 she was assigned to the base at Newport, Rhode Island, her first commanding officer being Lt-Cmdr W. M. Quigley. The *V-4* was named *Argonaut* on 19 February 1931 and after two years stationed in San Diego she was ordered to proceed to Pearl Harbor as her new base.

Argonaut leaves the splendour of Pearl Harbor for a peacetime patrol.

When the Japanese attacked she was at sea in the area of Midway in company with the USS *Trout* (SS-202) and both submarines were cruising on the surface that evening when they saw gun flashes in the direction of Midway Island. Lt-Cmdr Stephen G. Barchet the *Argonaut's* commander dived the boat and followed *Trout* towards the enemy force. With the enemy warships alert for any submarine attack, Barchet decided to play safe and take the *Argonaut* down to her operating depth of 300 feet and approach the enemy at slow speed. However, in that cautious early learning period the pursuer and pursued never caught sight of each other and *Argonaut* never got close enough to make an attack. A week later she heard three or four destroyers, but stayed deep and made no approach to the Japanese force. The lack of aggressiveness caused discontent in the boat and on return to Pearl Harbor the commanding officer was relieved of his duties.

From January to July 1942 *Argonaut* was at Mare Island Navy Yard, California for conversion to a transport submarine. This conversion was quickly put to use as she and *Nautilus* (SS-168) transported marines of Colonel Carlson's famed 2nd Marine Raider Battalion to make a daring raid on Makin Island in the Gilberts. *Argonaut* carried 121 marines while *Nautilus* carried a further ninety, leaving Pearl Harbor on 8 August for the raid on Makin which was purely diversionary as it was planned to create as much havoc as possible to disrupt the Japanese strategy in the area. The raid lasted from 17 to 19 August and was a complete success with the submarines landing the marines, waiting and then taking them off when the mission was completed. In the meantime both *Argonaut*, under the command of Lt-Cmdr John R. Pierce and *Nautilus* skippered by Lt-Cmdr William H. Brockman Jr, passed some of their waiting time by attacking shipping in the harbour.

Argonaut departed Pearl Harbor on 15 December 1942 for her third war patrol off New Britain and on 10 January 1943 she sighted a convoy of five ships escorted by three destroyers. Pierce bore in to the attack and hit a destroyer with a torpedo, but two others, the *Maikaze* and *Isokaze* immediately turned to attack the submarine with a savage depth-charging. The bow of the *Argonaut* broke surface and was heavily shelled by the destroyers until it disappeared beneath the waves.

This final action was witnessed by a US Army bomber returning to its base from a bombing raid. With its bomb racks empty the aircraft was helpless to assist and could only watch in horror as the boat went down — taking 105 crewmen with her. The *Argonaut* received three battle stars for her World War II service.

After conversion to a transport submarine *Argonaut* leaves Mare Island, California, 18 July 1942.

USS *Amberjack* (SS-219)

Amberjack was launched on 6 March 1942 by Mrs Randall Jacobs, wife of Rear Admiral Jacobs at the Electric Boat Company, Groton, Connecticut. She was placed under the command Lt-Cmdr John A. Bole Jr and commissioned on 19 June 1942.

She departed the submarine base at New London on 3 August 1942 heading for Pearl Harbor. After training and preparation for action she proceeded to her new base at Brisbane, Australia. *Amberjack* left Brisbane on 3 September to begin her first war patrol with orders to patrol the seas between New Ireland, New Britain and the Solomons.

On 18 September she fired four torpedoes at a transport, estimated at 7,000 tons, in a night surface attack with Bole reporting one hit. The following day she torpedoed and sank the 3,130-ton passenger/cargo *Shirogane Maru*. *Amberjack* was successful again on 7 October when, in a night surface attack, she sank the 2,101-ton store-ship *Senkai Maru* with two solid torpedo hits.

On 10 October she made a daring attack in Kavieng Harbor badly damaging the 4,861-ton naval cargo vessel *Tenryu Maru* and also scored hits on the oil tanker *Tonan Maru No.2*, a giant ex-whale factory ship of 19,262 tons. After two torpedo hits in the stern the latter sank into the mud with Bole claiming the tanker as sunk. The *Tonan Maru No.2* was refloated, towed to Japan for repairs and returned to service. However, she did eventually fall to a US submarine on 22 August 1944 when the USS *Pintado* (SS-387) sent her to the bottom forever. Remarkably, the *Pintado's* skipper, Lt-Cmdr Bernard A. Clarey had seen the *Tonan Maru No.2* before as he was executive officer on *Amberjack* in the attack on 10 October 1942.

After this excitement Bole was about to take the boat home when he received a radio signal ordering *Amberjack* to proceed to Espiritu Santo, New Hebrides. Once there he found that the desperate situation in the battle for Guadalcanal was deteriorating through a lack of aviation gasoline and *Amberjack* would be required to deliver 9,000 gallons of aviation fuel, 200 hundred 100-pound bombs and fifteen Air Corps personnel. A submarine on a 'special mission', under strict secrecy was nobody's friend with Bole having to evade Allied as well as enemy forces, and it was 25 October when she unloaded her precious cargo at Tulagi.

After an uneventful second war patrol she returned to Brisbane, departing again on 26 January 1943 for her third patrol. Her period in port had been cut short for operational reasons and the boat was not fully serviceable when she sailed.

The launch of *Amberjack* 6 March 1942.

Amberjack immediately before her commissioning and the long trip from New London to the Pacific.

On the afternoon of 3 February *Amberjack* sank a large schooner by gunfire and was in action again on the 4th in a night gun-battle with a 4,000-ton freighter. After one of the submarine's crew members was killed by fire from the freighter, Bole fired four torpedoes, the vessel sinking after a huge explosion. A post-war investigation failed to reveal the identity of this vessel.

On the night of 14 February *Amberjack* radioed that she had picked up a Japanese airman from the sea and had later been forced to submerge by the approach of two Japanese destroyers.

That was the last message received from *Amberjack* as she went down with all hands and the unfortunate Japanese aviator off New Britain after being depth-charged by the torpedo boat IJN *Hiyodori* accompanied by the submarine chaser *Ch.18*. A Japanese Navy patrol aircraft had located a submarine, bombed it and then guided the surface vessels to the spot.

After the war it was established that the Japanese warships collected a large amount of floating debris from the area, including a US Navy life-raft with the words 'Philadelphia Navy Yard' stencilled on it.

Amberjack was to be avenged! The *Hiyodori* was sunk by the USS *Gunnel* (SS-253) under the command of Lt-Cmdr Guy E. O'Neil Jr on 17 November 1944 while the *Ch.18* was destroyed by US aircraft on 30 December 1944.

Amberjack's service lasted just over six months, but who knows how many lives she saved on Guadalcanal with her brave dash. She received three battle stars in recognition of her short but valiant career.

USS *Grampus* (SS-207)

The submarine *Grampus* was launched on 23 December 1940 by the Electric Boat Company at Groton and commissioned on 23 May 1941 under the command of Lt-Cmdr Edward S. Hutchinson.

Grampus was in the Portsmouth Navy Yard, New Hampshire, at the time of the Japanese attack on Pearl Harbor. She departed on 22 December with orders to proceed to Pearl arriving on 1 February 1942. The boat did not have long to wait before going to war as she left on her first patrol on 8 February. She torpedoed and sank the *Kaijo Maru*, a tanker of 8,632 tons on 4 March and then continued her patrol of the Wotje and Kwajalein areas.

Her second and third war patrols out of Fremantle, Australia, were uneventful except for a night gun action with a Japanese patrol boat on 17 May when *Grampus* received a hit by a 3- or 4.7-inch shell in the after section of the conning tower fairwater, but no serious damage was done.

On 2 October *Grampus* sailed from Fremantle for her fourth patrol, this time under a new skipper, Lt-Cmdr John R. Craig. She carried four Coast-watchers that were successfully landed on Vella Lavella and Choiseul Islands even though these areas were heavily patrolled by the Japanese. On the 18th she claimed one torpedo hit on a light cruiser and also on this patrol she fired at a destroyer on 6 November. During this patrol *Grampus* was on the receiving end of some heavy anti-submarine activity having to withstand no fewer than 104 depth-charges in a number of attacks. She returned safely to Fremantle on 23 November 1942.

Her fifth war patrol began on 14 December and attacks were made on a freighter estimated at 6,000 tons and a destroyer on the 19th. On 10 January 1943 *Grampus* fired at two transports, one of 10,000 tons and the other of 8,000 tons and, although hits were claimed, these were never confirmed.

Grampus departed for her sixth war patrol on 9 February, but was ordered to return to Brisbane. On the 11th she sailed accompanied by the USS *Grayback* (SS-208), one of her sister ships, for the patrol on which *Grampus* was to disappear. Her orders were to sink any enemy vessels which were in transit through the Blackett Strait.

Japanese sources reported that a submarine, thought to be *Grampus*, torpedoed and damaged the 6,442-ton freighter *Keiyo Maru* on 19 February. A Japanese Navy Aichi E13A (Jake) seaplane of the 955th Air Group reported sinking a submarine on 19

Grampus wearing her number, 207, on 26 March 1941. This, of course, was deleted as the war clouds loomed.

Another view of above.

February, but *Grayback* reported a sighting of *Grampus* in her designated patrol area on 4 March.

The most likely cause of the loss of *Grampus* could have been the action of two Japanese destroyers, the *Minegumo* and the *Murasame*. The two were sunk by US surface ships on 6 March after conducting a supply mission to Japanese forces on Kolombangara and, after a large oil slick was sighted in the Blackett Strait where *Grampus* should have been, it can be assumed that the destroyers were responsible for the loss as they passed that way.

Grayback reported that she heard no depth-charging although she was only fifteen miles away, so another assumption is that *Grampus* was involved in gun action after being caught on the surface in the night of 5 March 1943.

The only definite fact is that John Craig and his seventy brave crewmembers were lost forever when *Grampus* went down with all hands. She was awarded three battle stars for her service and her name was struck from the Navy list on 21 June 1943.

USS *Triton* (SS-201)

Triton was launched by Mrs Ernest J. King, wife of Admiral King at Portsmouth Navy Yard, New Hampshire, on 25 March 1940. Her first commanding officer was Lt-Cmdr Willis A. Lent with commissioning taking place on 15 August 1940.

At the time of the attack on Pearl Harbor, *Triton* was patrolling off Wake Island and on 10 December Lt-Cmdr Lent claimed damage to a Japanese destroyer. She continued on patrol until the 21st when the submarine was ordered to proceed to Pearl Harbor, arriving on New Year's Eve giving *Triton's* crew a glimpse of the devastation from the Japanese attack.

Triton sailed for her second war patrol on 25 January 1942 heading for the East China Sea. On 17 February she fired four torpedoes at a freighter estimated at 6,000 tons and although one hit was claimed, conditions were unfavourable and the enemy vessel escaped. In the evening of that same day Lent made up for the earlier disappointment by sending the 1,498-ton *Shinyo Maru No.5* to the bottom. *Triton* was on target again on the 21st when she sank the 4,486-ton cargo ship *Shokyo Maru* with two torpedoes fired for two hits. She returned to Pearl on 17 March.

After overhaul and re-supply *Triton* got underway from the submarine base at Pearl Harbor on 13 April with a new commanding officer, Lt-Cmdr Charles C. Kirkpatrick. Her third war patrol was to take her back to the East China Sea. Ten days later she fired two torpedoes at a large trawler, but missed. However, not to be outdone, *Triton* battle-surfaced and destroyed the vessel, estimated at 1,000 tons, by gunfire. On 1 May she torpedoed and sank the 5,338-ton freighter *Calcutta Maru* and in the following three weeks Kirkpatrick caused havoc amongst the ranks of the Japanese. On the 6th she attacked a small convoy sinking the 2,208-ton *Taiei Maru* and the 5,665-ton *Taigen Maru*.

On 15 May she surfaced to destroy two 100-ton sampans with her deck gun. On 17 May 1942 *Triton* sighted a Japanese submarine on the surface in the waters to the south of Kyushu and although it was at a distance of 6,200 yards Kirkpatrick fired a single torpedo and got a perfect hit. The enemy submarine was the *I-64* which had departed from its base at Sasebo heading for Kwajalein. This boat was renumbered to *I-164* by the IJN on 20 May, but unknown to them, the Japanese submarine had already been sunk. *Triton* received a great welcome when she returned to Pearl Harbor on 4 June after a fine patrol.

Triton on a pre-war exercise.

Her fourth patrol took her to the Alaskan area and she departed on 25 June arriving on station on 3 July. She did not have long to wait for the action for on Independence Day she sank the Japanese destroyer *Nenohi* after patiently trailing it for ten hours. On the 28th and 29th she sighted two good-sized freighters, but heavy fog prevented successful attacks in both cases. An enemy submarine was sighted on 9 August, but as *Triton* prepared to attack, the hunter became the hunted as torpedoes from the Japanese boat forced her to go deep. *Triton* fired four torpedoes at a darkened vessel on the 15th and claimed one hit. The patrol ended on 7 September 1942 when she returned to Pearl Harbor for crew rest and an overhaul for the boat.

On 16 December she returned to action with a new type of assignment. She was to patrol an area between Midway and Wake Island, on duty to rescue aviators forced down into the sea after the strike against Wake. *Triton* was in company with the USS *Pike* (SS-173) and USS *Finback* (SS-230) and although no rescues were required, their presence gave the flyers great reassurance and, of course, lifeguard duty was to save many lives during the large Task Force missions and the B-29 raids against the Japanese homeland later in the war.

She gave herself an early Christmas present on the 24th when she sank the *Amakasu Maru No.1*, a Japanese Navy operated water tanker of 1,913 tons. After her special duties *Triton* was ordered to patrol the New Guinea-Rabaul-Truk area and *en route* she caught and sank the 3,394-ton cargo vessel *Omi Maru* on 28 December in a night torpedo attack. Torpedo malfunctions deprived her of a large tanker on 13 January 1943 when, off New Ireland, she hit the 10,182-ton *Akebono Maru* with one torpedo which exploded amidship, however, seven others fired perfectly, failed to detonate and the target escaped. On the 16th she scored hits on two cargo ships, but these could have been premature explosions of the torpedoes as both vessels proceeded on their way. Later in the day *Triton* fired three torpedoes at a large freighter, but without success. She was ordered to proceed to a new base at Brisbane, Australia, arriving there on 26 January.

On 16 February 1943 *Triton* departed Brisbane for her sixth war patrol, this time with a new skipper Lt-Cmdr George K. Mackenzie Jr. Her orders were to patrol between Rabaul and Shortland Basin and all was quiet until 6 March when *Triton* attacked a convoy, sinking the *Kiriha Maru*, a 3,057-ton cargo ship and damaged another, the 7,061-ton *Mito Maru*. The latter vessel escaped only to be sunk by the USS *Paddle* (SS-263) on 16 April 1944. In *Triton's* battle of the 6th she was forced to go deep by a malfunctioning torpedo which made a circular run. On 7 March she reported that she had fired torpedoes at two freighters, but an escorting destroyer had forced her to break off the attack.

Triton's last message was received on 11 March reporting that she was chasing a convoy. Messages sent to her received no reply and she was told to leave the area on 25 March and head home to Brisbane, but she never arrived.

Investigations of Japanese records after the war showed that a submarine was depth-charged and sunk north of the Admiralty Islands on 15 March and a great quantity of oil and debris came to the surface, including manufactured goods inscribed 'Made in USA'. In the area quoted there seems little doubt that the submarine was *Triton* and Mackenzie and his seventy-three-man crew went down fighting, leaving behind them a fine record. She received five battle stars for her actions.

Photographed from a US Navy Blimp during an exercise.

The Japanese destroyer *Nenohi* was a victim of *Triton* on Independence Day 1942.

George Mackenzie was *Triton's* aggressive young skipper.

USS *Pickerel* (SS-177)

Originally P-6, *Pickerel* later wore 177 until shortly before the outbreak of war.

The USS *Pickerel* was launched by the Electric Boat Company, Groton, on 7 July 1936 and, under the command of Lt L. J. Huffman was commissioned on 26 January 1937.

As war came to the Pacific, *Pickerel* headed towards Indo-China to conduct her first war patrol in the area of Cam Ranh Bay. She was in action on 19 December when her commander, Lt-Cmdr Barton E. Bacon Jr, fired five torpedoes at a Japanese patrol craft, but without success. *Pickerel* ended her first patrol on 29 December when she returned to Manila Bay, but it was a dangerous area at that time and she departed again on New Year's Eve.

On 10 January 1942 the submarine was on patrol between Manila and Surabaya when she sank the 2,929-ton armed cargo ship *Kanko Maru* with two torpedoes in a submerged night attack.

Pickerel's third and fourth patrols, were unsuccessful with Lt-Cmdr Bacon and his crew frustrated because they had seen nothing worth shooting at.

She was ordered to proceed to Pearl Harbor for a refit and departed Brisbane on 10 July. During the voyage she was to patrol in the Marianas and on 1 August she damaged a 4,800-ton freighter. This, her fifth war patrol ended on 26 August when she arrived at Pearl. She then headed for Mare Island Navy Yard, California, for her refit. After her refit *Pickerel* departed Mare Island on 22 December looking a little different having had her fairwater cut down forward and aft.

She commenced her sixth war patrol on 22 January 1943 with a new skipper. Lt-Cmdr Augustus H. Alston Jr, and orders to patrol in the Kuriles area. On 15 February *Pickerel* sank the 1,990-ton auxiliary vessel *Tateyama Maru* and on the 20th destroyed two sampans with gunfire. She returned to Pearl Harbor on 3 March.

Pickerel's seventh patrol started on 18 March 1943 when she left Pearl heading for Midway where she topped up her fuel tanks and departed for the northern coast of Japan on 22 March. The Japanese reported an attack on a submarine off Shiramuka Lighthouse, northern Honshu, on 3 April when naval aircraft bombed a submersible and then guided the *Shiragami*, a minelayer and the *Bunzan Maru*, an auxiliary submarine chaser, to the spot where the vessels dropped twenty-six depth-charges. The Japanese reported that a large quantity of oil floated to the surface. *Pickerel* was the only submarine in that area.

However, the post-war investigations of Japanese records show that the submarine chaser *Ch.13* was sunk by a submarine on 3 April and the 1,113-ton cargo ship *Fukuei Maru* was sunk in that area on the 7th, four days after the reported attack! If *Pickerel* did survive the depth-charging of the 3rd she was then lost to an unknown cause. Whatever the reason she was lost with all hands and taken off the Navy List on 19 August 1943.

Pickerel was awarded three battle stars for her operations.

At Mare Island Navy Yard on 22 December 1942, this photograph shows the changes made during the overhaul. External torpedo tubes fitted, the deck gun was moved forward and 20mm anti-aircraft guns were fitted fore and aft of the cut down conning tower.

Grenadier slides into the freezing Piscataqua River after launching at
Portsmouth Navy Yard, 29 November 1940.

USS *Grenadier* (SS-210)

Grenadier was launched at Portsmouth Navy Yard on 29 November 1940 by Mrs Walter S. Anderson, wife of the Director of Naval Intelligence. She was commissioned on 1 May 1941 with Lt-Cmdr Allan R. Joyce as commanding officer.

The submarine was being refitted in Portsmouth, New Hampshire, on 7 December 1941, but as soon as that was completed she headed towards the Pacific. *Grenadier's* first patrol from 4 February to 23 March 1942 proved fruitless after Joyce had taken her to operate off Honshu, Japan.

On 12 April *Grenadier* left Pearl Harbor for her second war patrol, this time under the command of Lt-Cmdr Willis A. Lent who joined her from the USS *Triton* (SS-201). She was ordered to the East China Sea and late in the afternoon of 8 May, Lent sighted a convoy consisting of a large passenger ship and six freighters. Being close to Kyushu and the possibility of air cover for the convoy, Lent made minimum use of the periscope, but concentrated his attack on the largest vessel. *Grenadier* fired four torpedoes at the passenger ship and, although all four were on target, only two exploded. However, this was enough to send the 14,457-ton *Taiyo Maru* to a watery grave and it was discovered after the war that this ship had been carrying Japanese scientists and other industrial experts to the East Indies to fully exploit the captured territory in that area. It's destruction cost the Japanese more than just one large vessel!

Almost immediately after firing, bombs from a patrolling aircraft exploded nearby and *Grenadier* went deep, soon depth-charges started to fall around her, but after some skilful handling and thirty-six explosions later, she came through without damage. Lent, along with other skippers, was concerned at the malfunctions but his report was rejected and US submarines went to sea once more with the offending Mark 14 torpedoes.

On the 25th she was ordered to join other submarines patrolling off Midway and took part in one of the famous sea battles of World War II when the Japanese fleet was soundly beaten by United States forces.

Lent's protests may have cost him command of *Grenadier* for she went to sea for her third war patrol with yet another skipper, Lt-Cmdr Bruce L. Carr. She was one of five submarines sent to patrol off the island of Truk during July and August of 1942. On 30 July *Grenadier* claimed to have sunk at 15,000-ton tanker, but this was never confirmed and she ended her unsuccessful patrol at Fremantle.

After a hurried refit *Grenadier* leaves Portsmouth for Pearl Harbor and the war, 27 December 1941.

She departed for her fourth war patrol on 13 October and on the 29th she laid thirty-two Mark 12 mines off the harbour of Haiphong, Indo-China. On 12 November she made a night attack on a freighter firing three torpedoes, but scored no hits. Malfunctions, once again, were a possibility as they seem to run directly under the enemy ship without exploding. This attack brought a swift response as *Grenadier* was severely depth-charged, but was able to escape.

However, damage to the batteries released chlorine gas making many of the crew suffer sickness and headaches. In the Makassar Strait on 20 November she sighted a Japanese aircraft carrier which she thought to be the *Ryujo*, but this was wrongly identified as this vessel had already been sunk by aircraft from the USS *Saratoga* (CV-3) on 24 August 1942. Nevertheless, it was an aircraft carrier and, although sadly out of range for an attack, *Grenadier* surfaced to radio the enemy's location in the hope that other Allied forces might be in a more favourable position.

Lt-Cmdr John A. Fitzgerald was the new commander as *Grenadier* departed Fremantle on New Year's Day 1943 to patrol the Java Sea.

In a gun action on 10 January she destroyed a sampan and two days later she sank two small cargo vessels also with her deck gun. On the night of the 22nd she scored two torpedo hits on a 7,000-ton freighter, but this ship was thought only to be damaged.

Her sixth, and what was to be her final, war patrol commenced on 20 March 1943 when she left the quiet comforts of Australia and headed for her assigned patrol area in the Strait of Malacca. On 21 April *Grenadier* sighted a two-ship convoy off the port of Penang on the west coast of Malaya, but after tailing the enemy vessels on the surface she was forced to crash-dive as a Japanese aircraft roared in to attack. Fitzgerald took her down to 130 feet when a tremendous explosion shook the boat sending *Grenadier* out of control until she hit the bottom at 270 feet. Leaks had started and fires in the electrical system were reported. The hull was damaged and dented and the propeller shafts were badly out of line. As darkness arrived the boat was brought to the surface and although the engines turned, the prop shafts were so much out of alignment that they would not turn. Fitzgerald hoped that once on the surface some of the problems could be solved, but it was worse than originally thought. Teams worked all through the night, but it was impossible to get the submarine to move. The desperate situation meant that once daylight came the boat would be dead in the water and an easy prey for the Japanese. Even a makeshift sail was rigged in attempt to get the *Grenadier* to move closer inshore.

Fitzgerald reluctantly decided to scuttle the boat after first destroying all secret equipment and papers. As this was in progress Japanese ships appeared and within minutes an enemy aircraft was diving in to attack the immobile submarine. However, *Grenadier* showed that she was not dead yet as her gunners opened up scoring hits on the aircraft but not before a bomb was dropped close aboard.

With the enemy surface ships closing in the crew abandoned the submarine with those who were sick going into the available rubber rafts. With the vents open the *Grenadier* began to go down by the stern. The Japanese ships circled the submarine, seemingly more concerned with photographing the event rather than picking up survivors. When the crew of the submarine was eventually rescued, they received the harsh treatment that, no doubt, they had expected.

The seventy-six were dispersed to prison camps and despite brutal treatment and near starvation all but four of the crew survived the ordeal including the skipper John Fitzgerald.

Grenadier received four battle stars for her service.

An unusual shot of *Runner* as she departs Portsmouth for sea trials on 16 October 1942.

USS *Runner* (SS-275)

Runner was launched at Portsmouth Navy Yard, New Hampshire, on 30 May 1942. Commander Frank W. Fenno Jr. took command, joining *Runner* after two successful war patrols as CO of the USS *Trout* (SS-202). *Runner* was commissioned on 30 July, but final completion was not until October. After a shakedown cruise from New London, she headed for the Pacific.

The submarine arrived at Pearl Harbor on 10 January 1943 and departed for her first patrol on the 18th. She was ordered to proceed to the area between Midway and the Palau Islands. Torpedo attacks were made on two freighters on 2 February, one on the 9th and on the other the 14th. On the 19th she fired three torpedoes at a 7,400-ton freighter, but none of these attacks were ever confirmed by the Japanese as sunk or damaged. It was during the last of these attacks that *Runner* herself was attacked by a Japanese aircraft which dropped a bomb while the boat was at periscope depth. The bomb detonated close to the port side of *Runner's* conning tower causing a great amount of damage throughout the submarine. She went down to 200 feet to escape any surface vessels which had been directed to the spot and was able to escape while her crew made emergency repairs. Due to the derangement of the periscopes, *Runner* had to terminate her patrol and return to Pearl Harbor, arriving on 7 March 1943.

She departed from Pearl Harbor for her second war patrol on 1 April with her primary task being to lay mines in the approach to Hong Kong harbour. This mission was carried out on the 20th when she laid thirty-two Mark 12 mines exactly to plan and with the mission completed she was to head for the Hainan Strait. On 24 April Commander Fenno sighted a freighter and an escort vessel zig-zagging and, after waiting for the best set-up, he fired three torpedoes, but heard only one explosion. Later, the Japanese claimed that the vessel, the 9,625-ton *Buenos Aires Maru*, as a hospital ship, but other records show this not to be so. *Runner* put into the base at Midway on 6 May 1943.

With a new skipper, Lt-Cmdr Joseph H. Bourland, *Runner* left Midway on 28 May 1943 for her third war patrol. She was to proceed to the coast of Hokkaido and spend one month patrolling the approaches to Orunato and Hakodate returning to Midway on 11 July. However, she was never heard from again, but the Japanese reported that two ships were lost in her patrol area as on 11 June the 1,338-ton freighter *Seinan Maru* and on 26 June a similar

A starboard view of *Runner*.

vessel of 4,935 tons, the *Shinryu Maru*, went down. If these were not lost to other unknown causes, *Runner* was the only submarine which could have destroyed them.

She was reported 'missing presumed lost' on 20 July 1943 and as Japanese records showed no anti-submarine activity in her area at that time, it is assumed that she was the victim of one of the many mines laid to protect the Hokkaido coast.

Whatever the reason, *Runner* and her seventy-eight crew were lost forever to an unknown cause. She received one battle star for her operations.

Lieutenant-Commander Joseph H. Bourland was lost with *Runner*.

USS *R-12* (SS-89)

The submarine *R-12* was launched by the Fore River Shipbuilding Company at Quincy, Massachusetts, on 15 August 1919 and commissioned on 23 September 1919.

After serving on training fleet exercises in the peacetime Navy, she was decommissioned and placed in reserve on 7 December 1932. As war loomed the *R-12* was returned to the active list and recommissioned on 1 July 1940.

Launch of the old *R-12* in 1919.

The New London Submarine Base was to be her home from 31 October 1941 and she operated patrols off the New England coast. On 20 February 1942 she was assigned to Guantanamo, Cuba, and the submarine operated between there and Key West, Florida. After a refit at New London in March and April 1943 she returned to Key West arriving there on 4 May.

The R-12 was given the task of training and it was on 12 June 1943 while making preparations to dive for a torpedo practice approach that the forward battery compartment started to flood. The collision alarm sounded and her skipper, Lt-Cmdr E. E. Shelby, who was on the bridge, immediately ordered all hatches closed and to blow main ballast, but it was too late as the boat went down in only fifteen seconds.

The six men on the bridge, including the commanding officer, were the only ones rescued while forty-two others including two Brazilian Navy officers, who were observing the exercise, were lost. Luckily, eighteen other crew-members were on liberty at the time the boat went down.

A Board of Inquiry concluded that the cause of the R-12's loss was not clear, but was probably due to the flooding of the submarine through a forward torpedo tube. This could never be confirmed as the boat sank in 600 feet of water, too deep for salvaging, or even investigation in those days.

The R-12's commanding officer, Lt-Cmdr Edward E. Shelby went on to skipper the USS Sunfish (SS-281) sinking over 45,000 tons of Japanese shipping in four highly successful war patrols.

USS *Grayling* (SS-209)

Grayling was launched at Portsmouth Navy Yard on 4 September 1940 and was commissioned on 1 March 1941 with Lt-Cmdr Elliot Olsen in command.

Tests and sea trials completed she was accepted by the Navy and departed from Portsmouth on 17 November 1941 assigned to the Pacific Fleet at Pearl Harbor. She was underway when the Japanese attacked and her entry into Pearl was delayed until Christmas Eve. As the newest vessel in port *Grayling* was selected for use in the change of command ceremony when, on 31 December, Admiral Chester W. Nimitz, assumed command of the Pacific Fleet and his flag was hoisted aboard the submarine.

The big day for *Grayling* as she is prepared for launch on 4 September 1940.

Grayling departed on 5 January 1942 for the first war patrol, but after searching the area north of the Gilbert Islands, she returned to Pearl Harbor on 7 March without making an attack.

On 27 March Olsen took the submarine out for her second patrol with orders to operate off the coast of Japan. She was a little more successful this time as she sank the 6,243-ton freighter *Ryujin Maru* in the Okinoshima area on 13 April. Apart from gun action against a sampan, there were no other attacks on this patrol and *Grayling* returned to Pearl Harbor on 16 May 1942.

As a strong Japanese force approached Midway Island all available resources were called upon to prevent an invasion. *Grayling* and a number of other submarines were called upon to report enemy movements. However, it was a PBY Catalina patrol aircraft which detected the first element of the Japanese force in the morning of 3 June and, later, when it was found that there were three groups converging on Midway some of the submarines, including *Grayling*, were ordered to attack.

History shows that it was air power which won the day in the Battle of Midway, but the submarines played their part in a number of ways and none more so than the old USS *Nautilus* (SS-168) which came across the damaged 17,500-ton aircraft carrier *Soryu* and sent it to the bottom with three torpedoes. *Grayling* herself came in for a harrowing time on 7 June when she was bombed by B-17s which reported her as a Japanese cruiser!

Grayling's third war patrol commenced on 14 July 1942 when she was ordered to operate near the heavily fortified island of Truk. On 13 August she claimed two torpedo hits on a freighter, estimated at 10,000 tons, but post-war records do not confirm this. A heavy fuel leak forced *Grayling* to return to base, arriving there on 26 August.

With repairs complete and a surface radar fitted *Grayling* departed for her fourth war patrol on 19 October. Truk was again the assigned patrol area, but this time she had a new skipper, Lt-Cmdr John E. Lee and on 10 November sank a 4,000-ton freighter to the south-west of the island. *Grayling* sank an enemy schooner by gunfire on 4 December before heading for her new base at Fremantle, Australia, where she arrived on 13 December 1942.

After spending Christmas and New Year on leave the refreshed crew took *Grayling* out on her fifth patrol on 7 January 1943. Her assigned area was off the Philippines coast and on the 26th of that month she intercepted the 479-ton steamer *Ushio Maru* and sank her with one torpedo. The crew took turns to watch through the periscope as the enemy vessel's bow broke away and the stern sank

Grayling on sea trials in March 1941.

first. The following day she fired three torpedoes at a passenger-cargo ship estimated at 4,500 tons and claimed two solid hits and a possible sinking, but this is not shown in Japanese records. On 11 February *Grayling* damaged the 6,032-ton cargo ship *Hoeison Maru* off Corregidor and sank a schooner by gunfire on 24 February before returning to Fremantle to end the patrol.

It was 18 March when the submarine left Australia, and for her sixth war patrol she was to cruise the Tarakan and Verde Island areas. *Grayling* was soon in action as, once again, she sank a schooner with her deck gun. On 9 April the boat tracked and sank the 4,103-ton cargo ship *Shanghai Maru* and later fired at a freighter of approximately 6,600 tons which was presumed sunk, but this was never confirmed.

On the 13th she was to engage in a night gun action with a 2,000-ton freighter which she thought had been destroyed, but Japanese records failed to add this vessel to *Grayling's* total. Yet another schooner was sunk on 18 April 1943. She ended her patrol on 25 April.

During her seventh patrol she claimed the sinking of an estimated 5,500-ton freighter in an underwater sonar attack on 7 June and on the 17th despatched a sampan in a night gun action. On 22 June *Grayling* was again in action when Lt-Cmdr Lee caught up with the 8,673-ton tanker *Eiyo Maru* and scored one torpedo hit, badly damaging the vessel. Her gun crew chalked up another sampan on the 25th.

Graylings eighth war patrol was under the command of Lt-Cmdr Robert M. Brinker and her first assignment was to deliver a ton of supplies and equipment to the guerrilla fighters at Pucio Point, Pandan Bay, Panay, on 31 July 1943. On 19 August she claimed to have damaged a 6,000-ton freighter and on the day after she destroyed a small oiler by gun action in the Sibutu Passage. She had a confirmed sinking on 27 August when the *Meizan Maru*, a cargo ship of 5,480 tons, was sent to the bottom. In between these actions, *Grayling* had delivered more supplies to the guerrilla force at Pucio Point.

On 9 September the Japanese passenger-cargo vessel *Hokuan Maru* reported sighting a submarine in shallow water west of Luzon in the Philippines and after a run over the area the enemy ship noted an impact with a submerged object which was, no doubt, *Grayling*. Her scheduled radio report on 12 September was not forthcoming and all attempts to reach her by radio failed.

It has been claimed that the Japanese submarine *I-182* was sunk by *Grayling* on 9 September, but these boats were operating in different areas. The claim was proved incorrect when records revealed that the *I-182* had been sunk by the destroyer USS *Wadsworth* (DD-516) south of Espiritu Santo, Solomon Islands on 1 September 1943.

Grayling received six battle stars for her operations and, perhaps, if records had been more accurate, her total of 20,575 tons sunk could have been doubled. There may be doubts about the way in which *Grayling* was lost, but however it happened, Robert Brinker and his seventy-five crew- members lie forever in the South China Sea.

USS *Pompano* (SS-181)

Pompano slid down the slipway at Mare Island Navy Yard on 11 March 1937 and was commissioned on 12 June 1937 under the command of Lt-Cmdr Lewis S. Parks, but trouble with her engines delayed delivery to the fleet.

At the time of the Japanese attack on Oahu *Pompano* was under way from Mare Island to Pearl Harbor reaching the base on 10 December. On the 18th, still under the command of Lew Parks she sailed from Pearl on her first war patrol to investigate Japanese defences in the Marshall Islands. It was to be the first American submarine reconnaissance mission of the war and, through Park's ingenuity, the periscope was adapted to hold a camera and *Pompano* became a pioneer in this type of photography. As if the operation was not hazardous enough, she was spotted by a PBY Catalina

Launched as P-10, *Pompano* is at Mare Island on 11 March 1937.

flying-boat on 20 December and bombed, fortunately without any damage. However, as the bomber departed three SBD dive bombers from the USS *Enterprise* (CV-6) attacked the submarine each dropping a bomb. The second bomb landed close aboard loosening rivets and causing a fuel leak which proved troublesome for the rest of the patrol. On 12 January 1942 she claimed three torpedo hits on a large freighter, but no sinking was recorded by the Japanese. On the 17th she fired two torpedoes at a patrol boat, but both of them exploded prematurely. The submarine completed her patrol and returned to Pearl Harbor arriving on 31 January.

Pompano's second patrol commenced on 20 April and, after calling at Midway to top-up with fuel, she arrived in her patrol area to the west of Okinawa and in the East China Sea on 7 May. On the 24th *Pompano* sank a fishing sampan in a night gun action and so on the day after sank the 902-ton oiler *Tokyo Maru* northwest of Naha. On 30 May she was in action again, this time sending the 7,983-ton transport *Atsuta Maru* to the bottom with two torpedoes. An escort vessel got a good fix on the submarine and dropped twenty-two depth charges before leaving the scene and a relieved American crew.

On 3 June she fired a torpedo at an inter-island steamer, but as this missed and the area was clear of other vessels *Pompano* surfaced and destroyed the enemy ship by gunfire. On 5 June a trawler, estimated at 100 tons, met the same fate. *Pompano* returned to Pearl Harbor, where she was due for a refit, on 18 June 1942.

The submarine departed for her third war patrol on 19 July and under a new skipper Lt-Cmdr Willis M. Thomas she headed for the coast of Japan. On 9 August she was heavily depth-charged by enemy destroyers, but the submarine was able to escape with minor damage. *Pompano* was in action on the 12th when she sank a 4,000-ton freighter and fired one torpedo at a destroyer. She sank the picket boat *Nanshin Maru* on 4 September with this vessel also being known as Naval Auxiliary No.163. Without further action *Pompano* arrived back at Pearl Harbor on the 12th.

She was ordered to Mare Island for a complete overhaul which included new engines, the cutting down of the fairwater and bridge area to mount additional 20mm guns and the moving of the three-inch deck gun to forward of the conning tower. *Pompano* sailed from the Navy Yard on 19 December and headed back to Pearl.

It was back to the war as she departed on her fourth patrol on 16 January 1943 and by the 25th she was patrolling off Kwajalein. Ordered to move to the Truk area *Pompano* damaged a large tanker

After a wartime overhaul and modifications, *Pompano* leaves California to return to action, 19 December 1942.

with two torpedoes on 30 January but an escort vessel prevented a further attack and only damage to the enemy ship could be claimed. She fired two of her stern torpedoes at a tanker on 4 February, but only one hit and the Japanese vessel was able to escape. On the 18th the submarine damaged a tanker with two hits, but an accurate depth-charge attack from escorting vessels forced *Pompano* to go deep. At the end of the patrol she returned, this time, to Midway arriving on the 28th.

Pompano sailed from Midway on 19 March and headed for the Tokyo Bay area on her fifth war patrol. For the whole period of this patrol she fought rough seas and stormy weather making the sighting of potential targets almost impossible. On 10 April the submarine did fire six torpedoes at what she assumed was an aircraft-carrier in a radar-guided night surface attack. The sound operator thought he heard two hits, but post-war Japanese records showed nothing of this action. She arrived at Pearl Harbor on 10 May after a frustrating patrol where the elements had come out on top.

Pompano was assigned to patrol the area off Nagoya, Japan, for her sixth war patrol and she departed on 6 June 1943. All was quiet until 4 July when she celebrated Independence Day by firing two torpedoes at the grounded seaplane tender *Sagara Maru*. The 7,189-ton vessel had been badly damaged by the USS *Harder* (SS-257) on 23 June. On 17 July *Pompano* gave her gun crew some practice when they sank a sampan estimated at 100 tons. On the 20th she fired two torpedoes at the 6,376-ton transport *Uyo Maru* in a submerged night attack, but it was thought that both had missed although explosions were heard. However, the post-war search of enemy records showed that the vessel was damaged in this attack. She ended the patrol at Midway on 28 July.

The veteran *Pompano* left Midway on her seventh patrol on 20 August with orders to proceed to the coastal waters off Honshu and Hokkaido, Japan. She was never heard from again, but Japanese records show a number of sinkings which could, due to their positions, be attributed to *Pompano*. On 1 September the 451-ton coaster *Nankai Maru* was sunk and on the 3rd the 5,600-ton transport *Akama Maru* was sent to the bottom. The 3,005-ton cargo vessel *Nanking Maru* was damaged in a torpedo attack on 9 September while on the 25th the 2,958-ton auxiliary vessel *Taiko Maru* was credited to *Pompano*, but this was later believed to have been sunk by the USS *Wahoo* (SS-238).

Thomas had orders to leave the patrol area on 27 September and take *Pompano* to Pearl Harbor for a refit. No transmissions were received from her after departure and as no anti-submarine attacks were reported in her area it is assumed that the submarine struck a mine and was lost with all hands in the area off northern Honshu. She received seven battle stars for her war service.

USS *Cisco* (SS-290)

The sixth boat in the new Balao-class, the *Cisco* was launched at Portsmouth Navy Yard on Christmas Eve 1942 and commissioned on 10 May 1943 with Commander James W. Coe in command. 'Red' Coe was a well-known skipper having successfully captained the submarines *S-39* (SS-144) and *Skipjack* (SS-184) earlier in the war and was rewarded by commissioning the new *Cisco*.

A builder's shot of *Cisco* dated 14 June 1943.

Cisco leaves for the war zone, but was lost soon after arriving.

Cisco arrived in Brisbane, Australia, on 1 September and then proceeded on coastal patrol duties until she put into Port Darwin on the 18th. With Coe anxious to get back into the war, she topped up with fuel and departed immediately on her first war patrol. However, the boat had a problem with the main hydraulic system and returned to port that same evening. With the system checked over and fixed *Cisco* sailed the following day. Nothing was ever heard from her again. Japanese records show that on 28 September 1943 one of their aircraft detected a submarine trailing oil and made a bombing run on the area of the source. The pilot then called in surface vessels to depth-charge the area producing even more oil and this continued to float to the surface even until 10 October. The area in Sulu Sea where the attack took place was the *Cisco's* patrol area and she was the only boat operating in that section.

Thus, a fighting skipper, a fine crew and a new submarine were lost before getting their chance to fight. However, *Cisco* was awarded one battle star for her service.

USS *S-44* (SS-155)

S-44 slid down the slipway at Bethlehem Shipbuilding Company at Quincy, Massachusetts on 27 October 1923 and was commissioned on 16 February 1925.

Until the attack which brought the United States into the war, *S-44* had served on a variety of training exercises, cruises and in a number of roles with the main fleet. As America's entry into the conflict seemed imminent she was one of a number of vessels selected for overhaul.

Her overhaul was completed at Philadelphia and after sea trials she departed for Panama on 7 January 1942. The *S-44* passed through the canal and conducted a security patrol in the Pacific approaches before she was ordered to Brisbane, Australia, where she arrived on 14 April. Under the command of Lt John R. 'Dinty' Moore the *S-44* had the luxury of air-conditioning, with the unit being bought by the Philadelphia shipyard workers and installed by her crew. With this innovation she was certainly the envy of the other 'Sugar' boat crews as temperatures in these older submarines sometimes reached unbearable levels, justifiably earning them the name 'Pigboats'.

On 23 April 1942 the *S-44* slipped her moorings from the submarine tender USS *Griffin* (AS-13), which was anchored at New Farm Wharf, near Brisbane, to get under way for her first war patrol. She was to patrol the area between New Britain and New Ireland, but just three days out, her port engine started to give trouble and had to be closed down. Then followed nearly thirty-six hours of backbreaking work before the engine could finally be restarted and the patrol resumed. On 9 May she sighted a Japanese destroyer, but with the enemy vessel's speed the *S-44* had little chance of making an attack.

Three days later she sighted an enemy cargo ship with an escort vessel and this time the set-up was perfect. Moore did not waste the opportunity as he sank the 5,644-ton *Shoei Maru* with three torpedoes. The Japanese escort craft immediately went after the *S-44*, but after some close depth-charge explosions she was able to escape her pursuer and head for home where she arrived on 23 May 1942.

The *S-44* was soon on the prowl again as she departed for her second patrol on 7 June. On 21 June she sank a converted gunboat, the 2,626-ton *Keijo Maru*, in an attack to the west of Gavutu. The enemy ship blew up with such ferocity that the submarine shook violently and this caused much internal damage and also attracted a Japanese aircraft to the spot. The enemy pilot was good, as the bomb he dropped exploded close to the conning tower causing a large amount of damage. Luckily only one bomb was dropped and she was able to slip away from the area. It was thought that the ship's explosion or the aircraft attack had also damaged her number one periscope, but when she surfaced to repair the damage it was found that a Japanese seaman's coat was firmly wrapped around the head of the periscope. The patrol was concluded on 5 July.

Her third patrol took the *S-44* to the Tulagi-Rabaul area after leaving Brisbane on 24 July 1942. On 10 August she sighted four Japanese cruisers in formation and she held her position as their track would eventually bring them within 900 yards of the submarine. As the cruisers arrived Moore fired four torpedoes at the nearest ship and all hit the vessel perfectly. The angry escorts then started an attack on *S-44*, but the depth-charging was erratic and she made good her escape. Her victim went down within minutes and it was later found to be the 8,800-ton *Kako* which, at that time, was the largest Japanese warship to be sunk by a US submarine. The *S-44* received a warm welcome on her return to Brisbane on 23 August and Moore was rewarded a Navy Cross.

Moore was also awarded by being given command of the USS *Sailfish* (SS-192) and the *S-44's* new CO was Lt-Cmdr Reuben Whitaker. Her fourth war patrol commenced on 17 September 1942, but on the following day she had a serious fire in the forward battery compartment, but this was extinguished without injury to crew members. Her patrol area off New Georgia proved to be a difficult operation with heavy enemy activity both at sea and in the air. On 4 October she claimed to have damaged a Japanese destroyer, but the following depth-charge attack on the *S-44* kept her submerged so no further observation could be made. On the 5th it seemed that the enemy had indeed inflicted some damage as she began taking-in water and as this became more serious she headed back to base returning on 14 October.

Whitaker was in line to command a fleet submarine and left the *S-44*, but no fleet boat became available and he received orders to report to the USS *Flying Fish* (SS-229) as executive officer. It was a bitter disappointment to him, but he was to go on to command the top-scoring submarine, USS *Flasher* (SS-249). The new skipper of *S-44* was to be Lt-Cmdr Francis E. Brown who had survived the grounding and loss of his previous command, the *S-39*.

The most successful of the old 'Sugar' boats, the *S-44*, is seen on its way to Philadelphia for wartime modifications.

The *S-44* was ordered to return to the United States for a complete overhaul and sailed for Philadelphia. On her return to the Pacific she was sent to Dutch Harbor in the Aleutians arriving there on 16 September 1943. On the 26th she departed Attu on her fifth, and what was to be her last, war patrol. The *S-44* was to patrol off Paramushiro and on 7 October a radar contact appeared to be a small merchant ship and Brown ordered battle surface.

On surfacing it was found that the target was not a cargo vessel after all, but the new escort ship *Ishigaki* which commenced firing with all guns. As the range closed Brown tried to submerge the *S-44*, but as the boat was hit many times and started to flood, abandon ship was ordered. One of the crew members opened the forward torpedo hatch and waved a white pillowcase as a sign of surrender, but the Japanese continued firing as the *S-44* went down. Lt-Cmdr Brown and fifty-five of his crew were lost with the boat, but by some miracle two Americans survived. Chief Torpedoman's Mate Ernest A. Duva and Radioman Third Class William F. Whitmore were picked up by the Japanese and received harsh treatment at the hands of their captors before being sent as forced labour in the Ashio copper mines. Both survived to relate the *S-44's* last moments before returning home at the war's end.

The *S-44* received five battle stars for war service and was avenged on 31 May 1944 when the USS *Herring* (SS-233) torpedoed and sank the *Ishigaki*.

Modifications completed, the *S-44* was photographed on 11 June 1943.

USS *Wahoo* (SS-238)

The *Wahoo* was launched on 14 February 1942 at the Mare Island Navy Yard, California, and commissioned on 15 May under the command of Lt-Cmdr Marvin G. Kennedy.

After its shakedown trials *Wahoo* arrived at Pearl Harbor on 18 August 1942. 'Pinky' Kennedy was a perfectionist who demanded relentless drills that brought the crew almost to the point of exhaustion, and it was no surprise when she was ordered to leave for her first war patrol just five days later. She was to patrol the waters around Truk and on 6 September Kennedy fired three torpedoes at an enemy freighter, but all missed as the vessel changed course. On the 20th four torpedoes were fired at an escorted freighter in a night attack, but only one hit was seen. However, the ship started to list to port then go down by the stern, but *Wahoo* could not stay around to watch the results of her work as the escort bore in to attack her. A rain squall came to her rescue and she was able to slip away. Kennedy claimed the sinking of a 6,500-ton freighter, but post-war records failed to confirm this. On 1 October she extended her patrol area to Ulul Island and sighted a few small boats, but as she was looking for bigger game the submarine let them pass. A few days later *Wahoo's* aims were almost achieved as along came a submariner's dream, the aircraft tender *Chiyoda* came into view and was unescorted. However, Kennedy never got into a good firing position and 11,000 tons of Japanese shipping passed by without even knowing that she was in danger. Next, another dream turned into a nightmare when an enemy aircraft-carrier escorted by two destroyers passed by with *Wahoo* again out of position to mount an attack. Kennedy identified this vessel as the *Ryujo*, but this ship had been sunk by carrier planes from the USS *Saratoga* (CV-3) a few weeks earlier. *Wahoo's* first patrol ended at Pearl Harbor on 17 October with Kennedy's lack of aggressiveness and skill being much criticized.

She departed for her second patrol on 8 November with Kennedy still in command, but only just. She was to proceed to the Bougainville area and on the 25th, without any good sightings, she moved to patrol the shipping lanes off Truk. On 10 December *Wahoo* contacted a three-freighter convoy escorted by a destroyer and Kennedy fired four torpedoes sinking the 5,355-ton *Kamoi Maru*. The destroyer immediately came in to attack and dropped 40 depth-charges, but none were close and Kennedy took *Wahoo* deep. On board the submarine was Lt-Cmdr Dudley W. Morton, known as 'Mush' to his colleagues, who was making the voyage as a PCO (Prospective Commanding Officer) and Lt-Cmdr Richard H. O'Kane, executive officer to Kennedy. Both urged him to attack again as they had a good chance of sinking another freighter and possibly the destroyer, but Kennedy did not want to risk further action and withdrew from the scene.

On 14 December *Wahoo* sighted a Japanese submarine with what appeared to be a number 12 on the conning tower. Kennedy fired three torpedoes and claimed to have sunk the submarine, but no enemy losses were reported in that area at that time. The patrol terminated at Brisbane on 26 December and on New Year's Eve Kennedy was relieved as skipper with 'Mush' Morton being given command of *Wahoo*. Kennedy went on to command the destroyer USS *Guest* (DD-472) and served with distinction on that vessel.

The names of *Wahoo* and Morton were to become legends in the annals of submarine warfare and he soon made his intentions known with a pep talk to his crew in which he stated that his patrols would be aggressive and if anyone did not like that idea they should seek an immediate transfer. Needless to say, nobody applied.

A number of changes and innovations were introduced in *Wahoo* with the most unusual being the use of his executive officer Dick O'Kane, to handle the periscope during an attack. In this way Morton could be getting an overall view of the set-up and give orders accordingly. It was good schooling for O'Kane who went on to make his own legend with the USS *Tang* (SS-306) and was rewarded with the Congressional Medal of Honor.

Morton took *Wahoo* out for the third patrol on 16 January 1943 and headed for the Wewak area on the North Coast of New Guinea. At the western end of Kairuru Island she sighted an enemy destroyer and a number of submarines at anchor, but as she closed in the destroyer started to get under way. *Wahoo* fired three torpedoes for one hit and Morton claimed to have sunk the vessel, but the destroyer *Harusame* did survive the attack although heavily damaged. However, it was later despatched by the Army Air Force on 8 June 1944. On 26 January she caught up with a four-ship convoy which consisted of two freighters, a tanker and a transport. In a battle lasting over ten hours *Wahoo* sank both freighters, the 1,901-ton *Fukuei Maru No. 2* and an unidentified 4,000-tonner, the troop-laden 5,447-ton transport *Buyo Maru* and badly damaged the 5,872-ton tanker *Pacific Maru*. The latter was repaired and returned to service only to be sunk by the USS *Guitarro* (SS-363) on 31 October 1944. The troop transport was literally full to its gunwales

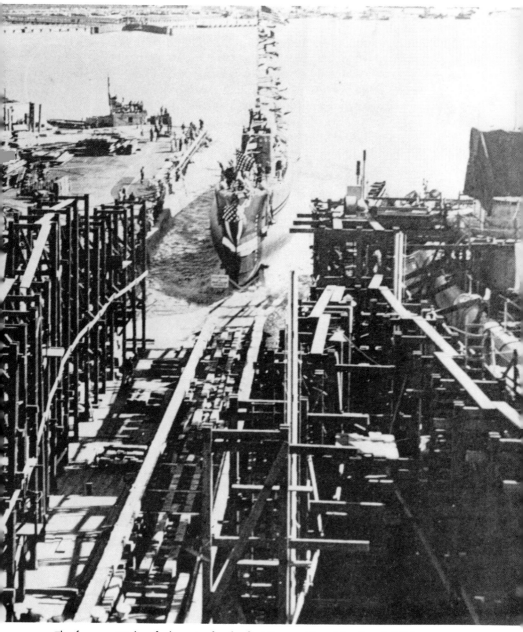

The famous *Wahoo* feels water for the first time at Mare Island on 14 February 1942. The USS *Whale* (SS-239) is under completion on the slipway to the right.

with Japanese soldiers on their way to New Guinea — Morton made sure that they never got there. With all torpedoes expended *Wahoo* headed back to base and after meeting a Japanese destroyer *en route*, Morton sent the famous message, 'Destroyer gunning, *Wahoo* running!' On 7 February 1943 she entered Pearl Harbor with a broom tied to her attack periscope indicating a clean sweep.

The new spirit which filled the whole crew was much in evidence during their stay at the Royal Hawaiian Hotel in Honolulu and they were in confident mood when *Wahoo* left Pearl Harbor for the beginning of her fourth war patrol on 23 February. Her operations area was to be the Yellow Sea and she opened her account for this patrol on 19 March when one perfect torpedo shot sank the 1,428-ton cargo ship *Zogen Maru*.

Just four hours later *Wahoo* attacked the 3,217-ton *Kowa Maru*, but only the first torpedo hit out of the four fired, with the second being a dud and the last two missing the target as the enemy vessel manoeuvred to avoid them. As on most occasions damaged vessels were repaired only to be sunk at a later date and the *Kowa Maru* was no exception as Sam Dealey's USS *Harder* (SS-257) sank it on 22 September 1943. The feeling of spring was really in the air on 21 March as 'Battle Stations Torpedo' was sounded and soon afterwards the 2,260-ton cargo ship *Hozan Maru* was slipping below the waves. A few hours later it was followed by the 2,183-ton *Nittsu Maru* after two torpedo hits. *Wahoo* surfaced for wreckage inspection collecting some interesting-looking ships' books and, of course, many souvenirs. On the 23rd one torpedo hit was enough to send a 2,400-ton cargo ship, reported as the *Katyosan Maru*, to the bottom. The following day *Wahoo* reported an attack on a tanker of approximately 7,500 tons and this was thought to have sunk although the submarine never received credit for this vessel. On 25 March she fired two torpedoes at the 2,076-ton cargo ship *Takaosan Maru*, but as these seemed to have no effect she sank the Japanese ship by gunfire. A similar fate awaited the 830-ton cargo vessel *Satsuki Maru* which provided the gun crew with some good target practice. On 27 March she attacked a small patrol craft leaving it ablaze and the following day *Wahoo's* 20-millimetre guns wrecked two motorized sampans. *Wahoo* was west of Yakujima on the 29th when she fired two torpedoes at the 2,556-ton freighter *Yamabato Maru* which went down in just two minutes. This action-packed patrol ended at Midway on 6 April 1943 as *Wahoo* entering the lagoon flying an Indian headdress battle flag with each feather representing an enemy ship sunk by the submarine.

Seen through *Wahoo's* periscope, the troop transport *Buyo Maru* goes down on 26 January 1943.

At 1500 hrs on 25 April *Wahoo* left Midway for her fifth war patrol and after making a photo reconnaissance of Matsuwa in the Kuril Islands she continued to patrol the area. On 4 May *Wahoo* went into action damaging a seaplane tender of the *Kamikawa Maru* class with one hit from a three torpedo spread — the second hit, but was a dud, and the third missed. The damaged vessel made off at 11 knots, but *Wahoo* required a battery charge and could not follow. On the 7th she was on target once again and this time one torpedo was enough to sink the 5,260-ton passenger/cargo *Tamon Maru No.5*. On the 8th three vessels, a large auxiliary and two freighters with the latter acting as escorts were detected zig-zagging on a course which would bring them within firing range of *Wahoo*. It was a good set-up and the submarine fired three torpedoes at the auxiliary, but disappointment was to follow as the first torpedo detonated half-way to the target, while the second was deflected by the explosion of the first and the third hit exactly at the aiming point, but failed to explode. Both escorts charged in to attack *Wahoo*, but some skilful handling of the boat left the depth-charges exploding well astern. On the following day the 3,204-ton cargo *Takao Maru* and a similar vessel of 1,912 tons, the *Jinmu Maru* were both sent to the bottom with single torpedo hits. On 12 May *Wahoo* fired two torpedoes at each of two freighters for one hit. The submarine tracked the ships and shortly after midnight fired another torpedo at the damaged freighter which was trailing well behind the first, but this missed and it was left to the last torpedo, which was in the stern tubes, to hit perfectly. *Wahoo* was about to finish off the ship by gunfire, when the first freighter commenced firing with an accurate pattern and Morton decided that making sure the sinking vessel did go down was just not worth the chance of losing *Wahoo*. The submarine returned to Pearl on 21 May 1943 and, once again, a great welcome awaited her. The next day Admiral Chester W. Nimitz, Commander-in-Chief Pacific Fleet, awarded Morton a second Navy Cross at a ceremony held on *Wahoo*.

She then received orders to proceed to Mare Island Navy Yard for a complete overhaul and left Pearl Harbor on the 24th. After the overhaul *Wahoo* returned to Pearl Harbor on 27 July 1943 looking a completely different boat with the conning tower fairwater being cut down and appearing much more like the Balao class submarines which were then coming off the slipways at the rate of five a month. Dick O'Kane had left the *Wahoo* to take command of one of these new boats, the USS *Tang* (SS-306), which was soon to write its own chapter in the history books. *Wahoo's* sixth war patrol began on 2 August with orders to patrol the Sea of Japan and the Sea of Okhotsk, but this patrol was to be a great disappointment as all torpedoes fired turned out to be duds, exploded prematurely or made erratic runs. Out of the twelve Japanese vessels sighted nine were tracked and fired at and although hits were made no damage was done. *Wahoo* was ordered to return to base after Morton's blistering messages reported failure after failure and the patrol terminated at Pearl on 29 August.

Torpedoes had been so unreliable since the commencement of hostilities in the Pacific so that Morton must have felt confident as *Wahoo* departed from Pearl on 9 September 1943 for her seventh patrol for she carried a full load of twenty-four of the still classified Mark 18 electric torpedoes and the submarine was to proceed into the Sea of Japan. The USS *Sawfish* (SS-276) would follow in a few days time. Around the 20 September *Wahoo* entered its patrol area through La Perouse Strait and her orders were to leave at sunset on 21 October reporting clear after passing through the Kurils. No message was ever received, but such was the faith in Morton and his ship that she was not reported overdue until 2 December.

Japanese records show that *Wahoo* sank the 1,238-ton cargo vessel *Masaki Maru* on 29 September. On 5 October the Japanese News Agency Domei reported that a United States submarine had sunk the 7,903-ton steamer *Konron Maru* off the west coast of Honshu with the loss of 544 of its passengers and crew. On the 6th she sank a freighter of 1,283 tons and on 9 October she sent the 2,995-ton cargo vessel *Kanko Maru* to the bottom.

Wahoo's fate seems to have been sealed on 11 October when an enemy shore battery which overlooked Soya Strait, fired at a surfaced submarine and claimed a number of hits before the boat dived. The battery commander reported the incident and an aircraft was sent from Ominato. At 0920 hrs it detected an oil patch and the shadow of a conning tower with this shape being bombed. The aeroplane called for assistance and circled the spot until other aircraft arrived. A submarine was positively identified and more bombs were dropped until surface ships appeared including the Submarine Chasers 15 and 43 which dropped depth-charges; the former vessel identified part of a ship's propeller being thrown up by one of the explosions. Another aircraft arrived as did Auxiliary Minesweeper 18, but nothing more was seen.

Admiral Nimitz awards 'Mush' Morton his second Navy Cross. 22 May 1943.

'Mush' Morton and his valiant crew were gone, but *Wahoo's* record stands proudly in the history of submarine warfare. Reliable torpedoes on that disastrous sixth patrol could well have made *Wahoo* the top-scoring US submarine. She received six battle stars for her war service.

Wahoo after overhaul at Mare Island. This is one of the last known photographs to be taken of her.

USS *Dorado* (SS-248)

Dorado was launched by the Electric Boat Company at Groton, Connecticut, on 23 May 1943 and with Lt-Cmdr Earle C. Schneider in command, she was commissioned on 28 August 1943.

After trials, *Dorado* left New London on 6 October 1943 with orders to proceed to the Canal Zone and then into the Pacific. She was scheduled to arrive at Panama on the 14th, but when the submarine did not appear an air and sea search was immediately started. A large oil slick and floating debris were all that was found.

Great things were expected of *Dorado* as she was launched on 23 May 1943, but she was destined never to get into the fight.

A number of possibilities exist for her loss, but the most likely seems to have been that *Dorado* was bombed by a PBM Mariner flying-boat from Guantanamo Air Station, Cuba. A Court of Inquiry revealed that the aircraft bombed an unidentified submarine on 12 October, but due to a lack of evidence it was unable to come to a definite conclusion. If the Mariner did bomb *Dorado* one of them must have been well off course, but it also was not unusual for aviators to disregard safety areas in their enthusiasm to have a successful patrol.

Other causes were put forward including striking one of the mines laid in the area by the German submarine *U-214*, or an operational loss, but whatever misfortune overtook *Dorado* it remains indisputable that she was a new boat with an eager crew who never got the chance to get into the action.

Earle Schneider, commander of the ill-fated *Dorado*.

Electric Boat Company workers putting the finishing touches to *Dorado*. Apart from the launching shot, this is the only known photograph of her.

This photograph is the only existing picture of *Corvina (SS-226)*.

Corvina's crew at the commissioning party.

USS *Corvina* (SS-226)

The Electric Boat Company launched *Corvina* on 9 May 1943 with the ceremony being carried out by Mrs Christie, wife of Admiral Ralph W. Christie, Commander of Submarines in the Southwest Pacific. The submarine was commissioned on 6 August 1943 with Commander Roderick S. Rooney as captain. Departing from New London on 18 September, *Corvina* had an uneventful passage arriving at Pearl Harbor on 14 October.

Her first war patrol commenced on 4 November when she proceeded to Johnston Island to top-up her tanks calling in there on the 6th. *Corvina* departed immediately heading to her patrol station south of Truk where, with other submarines, she was to take part in 'Operation Galvanic' with the capture of Tarawa and other outposts in the Gilberts being the major objective. Their mission was to intercept and attack any enemy vessels which might arrive to defend the islands. *Corvina* along with sister ships *Blackfish* (SS-221) and USS *Drum* (SS-228) were advised that a Japanese submarine was heading through their patrol area and was to be intercepted. After that a certain amount of confusion must have crept in as each American submarine was aware of each other's presence and had to be absolutely positive of identification before making any attack. *Blackfish*, in fact, saw a submarine but could not identify it as Japanese so did not fire at the vessel. However, *Corvina* was never heard from or seen again.

Post-war Japanese records show that one of their submarines, the *I-176* under the command of Lt-Cmdr K. Yamaguchi, sank an American submarine on 16 November. They caught it on the surface and fired three torpedoes which were reported to have resulted in a large explosion.

Corvina is the only United States submarine known to have been sunk by a Japanese submarine and her loss with the eighty-two crew members was announced on 23 December 1943.

USS *Sculpin* (SS-191)

Sculpin was launched at Portsmouth Navy Yard on 27 July 1938 by Mrs J. R. Defrees and commissioned on 16 January 1939 with Lieutenant Warren D. Wilkin in command.

While on her shakedown cruise she was ordered to search for her sister submarine *Squalus* (SS-192) which had sunk during a test dive off Portsmouth on 23 May. *Sculpin* located the sunken vessel, established communications and remained on station until the rescue ship USS *Falcon* (ASR-2) arrived. The *Squalus* was eventually refloated, given the new name *Sailfish* and went on to highly successful wartime service.

As the war in the Pacific started, *Sculpin*, now under the captaincy of Lt-Cmdr Lucius H. Chappell, departed Cavite in the Philippines on 8 December 1941 to escort the USS *Langley* (AV-3), a seaplane tender which had been converted from the Navy's first aircraft-carrier and the oiler *Pecos*, safely to the San Bernadino Strait. Along with the submarine USS *Seawolf* (SS-197) it was the beginning of their first war patrol with the assigned area to be north of Luzon. On the night of 10 January 1942 she intercepted a two-ship convoy and claimed hits on a cargo vessel estimated at 5,000 tons. *Sculpin's* patrol ended when she entered Surabaya, Java, on 22 January.

Her second war patrol started just eight days later with orders to patrol the Molucca Sea. On 4 February she put two torpedoes into the Japanese destroyer *Suzukaze* which had to beach itself to prevent from sinking. The enemy destroyer eventually fell to a US submarine when it was sunk by the USS *Skipjack* (SS-184) on 26 January 1944.

On 6 February *Sculpin* fired two torpedoes at a Japanese light cruiser in a night surface attack and Chappell was convinced that they had both struck home. However, they must have been premature as Japanese records showed no damage to the cruiser. On the 17th she was detected by an enemy destroyer and a heavy depth-charging resulted in damage to the starboard main controller and the starboard propeller shaft. She was advised to proceed to Exmouth, Australia, for repairs.

Sculpin was ready for sea and after calling at Fremantle she departed on her third patrol on 13 March 1942. While once again patrolling the Molucca Sea she fired torpedoes at a number of targets, but achieved nothing as the malfunctioning torpedoes either ran wild, failed to explode or exploded too early. In any event it spelled frustration for *Sculpin* and her crew and the patrol was terminated at Fremantle on 27 April.

She was assigned to the South China Sea for her fourth patrol which commenced on 29 May. On 13 June she torpedoed a cargo vessel estimated at 4,000 tons and on the 14th she fired torpedoes at two tankers each of approximately 8,000 tons. On the 18th her target was a 7,000-ton freighter, but all of these actions went unrecorded by the Japanese. *Sculpin* returned to Australia on 17 July.

Her fifth patrol took her to the Bismark Archipelago after leaving Fremantle on 8 September. For nearly three weeks no sightings were made, but on the 28th she scored two hits on the Seaplane Tender *Nisshin*, a vessel of 11,317 tons which had only been completed in February of that year. *Sculpin* could not confirm the amount of damage as she had to go deep as two escorts came in to attack. The first depth-charges exploded as the submarine was at 250 feet and then followed a four-hour ordeal which caused a great amount of damage including the temporary loss of main power and loss of control.

Sculpin seen soon after completion in January 1939.

Sculpin was able to escape the enemy vessels and temporary repairs proved good enough to keep her on patrol. Chappell's decision to stay on patrol paid off for on 7 October she torpedoed and sank the 4,731-ton transport *Maminoue Maru* and on the 14th a tanker, the 1,921-ton *Sumiyoshi Maru*, went to the bottom after a night surface attack. On the 18th *Sculpin* claimed two hits on a cargo ship estimated at 4,000 tons, but this was not confirmed in post-war records. This patrol terminated on 26 October.

Sculpin's operational base was now Brisbane and she departed there for her sixth war patrol on 18 November heading for Truk. On 11 December she was bombed by Japanese aircraft, but as she dived to escape, the explosions were heard to be well off target. After receiving an Ultra message from base *Sculpin* went after an enemy aircraft carrier on the night of the 18th and, on the surface, closed to within nine miles of the enemy, before she was attacked by two destroyers. One of the Japanese escorts caught her in its searchlight and both enemy vessels opened fire forcing Chappell to take her down rapidly. A depth-charge attack followed but, once again, *Sculpin* was able to evade. The night after she attacked a tanker of approximately 7,500 tons and damaged it with two torpedoes. *Sculpin* was ordered to end the patrol at Pearl Harbor and she arrived there on 8 January 1943. She then proceeded to Mare Island for an overhaul which was to take over three months.

The submarine was like new as she passed the Golden Gate Bridge heading for Pearl where *Sculpin* tied up at the submarine base on 9 May. Eager to get back into the war *Sculpin* left Pearl Harbor for her seventh patrol on 24 May and set course for Honshu.

While operating near the rock-formed island of Sofu Gan on 9 June she made contact with targets later identified as two carriers and a cruiser, but *Sculpin* was not in a position to attack and even at flank-speed she could not close on the enemy force. More in hope than anything, Chappell fired four torpedoes at a range of 7,000 yards, but no hits resulted. It has been reported that in this attack *Sculpin* hit and damaged the carrier *Hiyo*, but this has been confused with the successful attack by USS *Trigger* (SS-237) on the 10th. On 14 June *Sculpin* put one torpedo into a 4,500-ton cargo ship, but was forced to go deep to escape the angry escorts. On the 19th her deck gun destroyed the 79-ton picket boat *Miyasho Maru No. 1* and, later on the same day, sank the 135-ton cargo ship *Sagami Maru*. *Sculpin* put in to Midway to end the patrol on 4 July.

The eighth war patrol commenced on 25 July and her assigned operations area was to be off the coast of China and in the Strait of Formosa. On 9 August she sent the 3,183-ton cargo ship *Sekko Maru* to the bottom with one torpedo hit. Then followed two attacks on cargo vessels, but malfunctioning torpedoes allowed both ships to continue unharmed. On her way home *Sculpin* made a reconnaissance of Marcus Island before returning to Midway on 17 September after a patrol lasting 55 days.

Then followed a short period of overhaul at Pearl Harbor before leaving on 5 November to patrol to the north-east of Truk. After

In her final form, with changes to the conning tower, *Sculpin* leaves Mare Island in May 1943.

refuelling at Johnston Island on the 7th she proceeded to her assigned station. Her ninth war patrol, this time under the captaincy of Cmdr Fred Connaway was to be a part of 'Operation Galvanic' operating with USS *Searaven* (SS-196) with their mission being to intercept any Japanese vessels which operated from Truk during the Gilbert Islands campaign. On board *Sculpin* was Captain John P. Cromwell who was to be wolf-pack commander if USS *Apogon* (SS-308) and USS *Spearfish* (SS-190) joined the small group.

Captain Cromwell was a senior officer who was involved in the planning of 'Operation Galvanic' and was an expert on Ultra, the priority message-containing information received from decoded Japanese transmissions. On the night of 18 November 1943 *Sculpin* made radar contact with a large convoy and shadowed the enemy until the following morning when she prepared to attack, but look-outs on the Japanese ships spotted *Sculpin's* periscope. The escorts were quickly on the scene and the first depth-charge attack caused only minor damage, but the second attack caused more damage keeping *Sculpin* under for several hours. Connaway decided to take the boat to periscope depth, but as *Sculpin* was rising the depth gauge stuck at 125 feet and the young diving officer Ensign W. Maxwell Fiedler did not realize this in time and the boat broke surface. As the submarine broached the Japanese destroyer *Yamagumo* attacked immediately forcing Connaway to order a crash-dive. This time the destroyer was right on target and the eighteen depth-charges dropped by *Yamagumo* caused serious damage making *Sculpin* uncontrollable and bad leaks forced Connaway into a decision to battle-surface and try to fight it out by a gun action. With the odds stacked high against them *Sculpin's* brave crew quickly engaged the enemy warship, but the fight was too one-sided. *Yamagumo's* first salvo hit the submarine's bridge instantly killing Cmdr Connaway, his executive officer, Nelson J. Allen and gunnery officer Joseph R. Defrees Jr, son of Rear-Admiral Defrees and whose mother had launched *Sculpin* five years earlier. Command of the boat passed to Lt G. E. Brown Jr, a young reserve officer who, as the fight was hopeless, ordered the *Sculpin* to be scuttled and for the crew to abandon ship. The vents were opened and she started to go down still under fire from the *Yamagumo*. Captain Cromwell told Brown that he would go down with *Sculpin* as he knew too much of 'Galvanic's' plans and of the code-breaking Ultra and was sure that the Japanese would extract this information through torture. Ensign Fiedler also elected not to leave her and probably felt responsible for the disaster.

Twelve men in all decided to ride *Sculpin* down. It was just eleven minutes from surfacing until she slid beneath the waves. The Japanese picked up just one-half of the complement, Brown and forty-one others, but immediately threw a badly injured American back into the sea and another just avoided this fate by breaking free and joining his colleagues. After interrogation and the kind of treatment they expected, they were separated into two groups for transportation to Japan. The aircraft-carriers *Chuyo* and *Unyo* were to carry the submariners with twenty-one on the first carrier and twenty on the latter.

There was to be an ironic ending to the story as on 4 December the 20,000-ton *Chuyo* was sunk by the USS *Sailfish* (SS-192) and twenty prisoners from the *Sculpin* were lost with the enemy ship. One of the Americans escaped and was able to catch hold of a ladder on a Japanese destroyer and haul himself aboard. By a strange twist of fate it was *Sculpin* which, four and a half years earlier had located the sunken submarine *Squalus* which was later raised and renamed *Sailfish*!

At the war's end twenty-one survivors of *Sculpin* returned to give an account of her last action and of the supreme sacrifice of Captain Cromwell who was posthumously awarded the Congressional Medal of Honor for this act of heroism and devotion to his country. *Sculpin* herself was awarded eight battle stars for her service in World War II.

USS *Capelin* (SS-289)

Capelin was launched at Portsmouth Navy Yard on 20 January 1943 and was commissioned on 4 June under the captaincy of Lt-Cmdr Elliot E. Marshall. She was fifth in the Balao-class and was placed under the command of 'Steam' Marshall when his previous boat, the old USS *Cuttlefish* (SS-171), was transferred to training duties after three war patrols in the Pacific.

Capelin left New London's drizzle on 3 September 1943 for the warmth of Brisbane, Australia, as she had been assigned to the Submarine Force, Southwest Pacific.

Her first war patrol started at Darwin on 30 October with orders to rescue the crew of a B-24 Liberator bomber which had crashed in the Celebes area, but *en route* this order was cancelled and she assumed a normal patrol in the Molucca Sea. On 11 November an intelligence report alerted Marshall to a small convoy escorted by two destroyers and *Capelin* went in to attack. Sadly, malfunctioning torpedoes deprived her of a larger score, but she was able to sink the 3,127-ton cargo ship *Kunitama Maru* to the northwest of Ambon Island. *Capelin* returned to Darwin on the 16th with a defective conning tower hatch, bow plane and a malfunctioning radar tube.

Capelin at speed during her trials off New London in August 1943.

All of these problems were quickly attended to and she sailed from Darwin the following day proceeding on her second patrol in the Molucca Sea. The patrol could extend to the Celebes Sea searching for targets around the Moratai Strait, Davao Gulf and the Sarangani Islands and also investigating Kaoe Bay and Halmahera. On 2 December Lt-Cmdr Tom Hogan in USS *Bonefish* (SS-223) sighted a submarine, which he thought was *Capelin*, about five miles away and this boat had obviously seen *Bonefish* as it dived immediately.

Hogan's submarine had been attacking a convoy and he was anxious to pass a message to *Capelin* to advise them of this and to attack any stray vessels. Hogan sent the message by sonar giving Marshall's nickname 'Steam' and this was acknowledged by the other submarine.

That was the last anyone saw or heard of *Capelin* as she was lost with all hands. The cause of her disappearance will remain a mystery as no Japanese anti-submarine action was reported for that time and in that area. There were minefields in the area, but most were known and Marshall would have stayed clear. The other possibility is an operational loss caused by one of the problems previously encountered, or by a later one, but there are no definite conclusions.

Whatever the cause *Capelin* and the seventy-eight brave crew members lie forever in the deep. She received one battle star for her war service.

Elliot 'Steam' Marshall was *Capelin's* popular commander.

USS *Scorpion* (SS-278)

Another Portsmouth Navy Yard boat was the *Scorpion* which, on 20 July 1942, was part of the yard's first double launching as she followed the USS *Scamp* (SS-277) into the Piscataqua River. Lt-Cmdr William N. Wylie was in command when *Scorpion* was commissioned on 1 October 1942.

Scorpion with launching celebration well under way. A Navy tug stands by.

Based at Pearl Harbor, she departed for her first war patrol on 5 April 1943 with orders to lay mines off the coast of Honshu. This task was successfully completed on 19 April when she laid twenty-two mines off Inubo Saki and on the following day she destroyed her first enemy vessel when she sank the 1,934-ton converted gunboat *Maiji Maru* off Kinkazan. In the following three days she destroyed four sampans by gun action and with one torpedo damaged a freighter estimated at 7,500 tons. On the 27th four torpedoes deprived the Japanese of the 6,380-ton passenger/cargo ship *Yuzan Maru* with *Scorpion* going into attack on a four-ship convoy escorted by a Shigure-class destroyer. *Scorpion* was carrying a new device known as a Bathothermograph or BT which measured the temperature of the surrounding water and assisted the commander to seek colder water distorting enemy anti-submarine sonar pinging. Wylie used this to the full and the eight depth-charges dropped by the escort were not accurate. On the evening of the 28th she was ordered to head for Midway, but on the way *Scorpion* destroyed a 100-ton patrol vessel with her deck gun. On the 30th when she was about 600 miles from Japan the submarine sighted what appeared to be a small freighter, but as it approached it was seen to be a well-armed patrol boat of around 600 tons. As the vessels engaged in surface action *Scorpion's* deck gun jammed after only fifteen rounds and Wylie took her out of range until the gun was cleared. She then returned to open fire on the Japanese ship with the deck gun and other small arms, but after the gun jammed a number of times and the enemy ship, despite heavy damage, showed no signs of sinking Wylie turned the submarine and fired one torpedo from 500 yards.

This hit the enemy amidships with a tremendous explosion and the patrol boat, which turned out to be the *Ebisu Maru*, went down with guns still firing and the Rising Sun flag still flying. It was during this action that the *Scorpion's* executive officer, Lt-Cmdr Reginald M. Raymond, who was manning a Browning automatic rifle on the submarine's bridge was killed by enemy gunfire. This was a great tragedy as 'Reggie' Raymond was a fine officer and was expected to take command of the USS *Runner* (SS-275) when the patrol was completed. The *Scorpion* was preparing a burial at sea for Raymond when a Japanese aircraft attacked forcing her to dive and dropping two-depth charges astern. Lt-Cmdr Raymond's body was lost during the dive, but the formal service was carried out later that evening. His death caused great sadness amongst the crew of *Scorpion*. In January 1944 the destroyer escort USS *Raymond* (DE-341) was named in his honour. *Scorpion* arrived at Pearl Harbor on 8 May 1943.

Her second war patrol commenced on 29 May and after a call at Midway for fuel on 2 June, she headed for the Yellow Sea. On 3 July she sighted a five-ship convoy and after firing at the overlapping targets, the escorts attacked and she had to go deep, but in the shallow waters *Scorpion* hit the bottom at only 90 feet wiping off her sonar sound heads. She was later credited with the sinking of the 3,890-ton freighter *Anzan Maru* and the 6,112-ton passenger/cargo vessel *Kokuryu Maru*, but because of damage received had to return to Midway and tied up to the submarine tender USS *Sperry* (AS-12)

After commissioning, *Scorpion* leaves Portsmouth, New Hampshire, for her sea trials.

on 15 July. Repairs to *Scorpion* were completed at Midway and she took part in a short training exercise before her third patrol, but after a submerged practice attack she surfaced only to run aground on the coral which practically surrounded Midway. A tug was required to pull *Scorpion* off the reef, but it was nearly five hours before she became free. This time the damage was so bad that *Sperry* could not handle it and the submarine headed back to Pearl for repairs and refit arriving there on 26 July 1943.

The docking took longer than expected because *Scorpion* did not leave Pearl Harbor until 13 October with a new skipper, Commander Maximilian G. Schmidt taking her out for her third war patrol. After the usual call at Midway she headed for the Marianas to search out targets in that area. On 3 November she sighted a Mogami-class cruiser, but bad weather with heavy rain squalls spoilt the attack as she could not get into a good firing position. On the 8th *Scorpion* went after what appeared to be a freighter, but this turned out to be a heavily armed 'Q' ship which manoeuvred into a position to attack the submarine and Schmidt decided to leave the area. On the 13th she detected a convoy which consisted of a freighter, a tanker and three escorting warships. Schmidt put one torpedo into the tanker before one of the escorts caused him to break off the attack and after depth-charging for a short period the enemy vessel returned to the convoy. It was later learned that the tanker, the 14,050-ton *Shiretoko Maru* had to be towed to Singapore and took no further part in Japan's war effort. It is interesting to note that the *Shiretoko* had been damaged in a torpedo attack by the USS *Permit* (SS-178) exactly two months earlier and this was the tanker's first voyage after repairs. *Scorpion* ended the patrol at Pearl Harbor on 5 December.

After spending Christmas in the comfort of the Royal Hawaiian Hotel in Honolulu the crew of the *Scorpion* were refreshed and ready for action as the boat headed out from Pearl on 29 December. After a fuel top-up she departed Midway on 3 January 1944 to proceed to the East China and Yellow Sea areas. In the morning of the 5th, Schmidt radioed that a crew member had badly fractured his arm and requested a rendezvous with the USS *Herring* (SS-233) which was returning to Midway at the end of a patrol. The meeting was made, but heavy seas prevented the injured man from being transferred and Schmidt reported that they would continue to their patrol area.

Scorpion was never seen again and it is possible that she hit one of the mines laid at the entrance to the Yellow Sea, but that is only an assumption. Where she lies remains unknown and she was reported lost on 6 March 1944. Three battle stars were awarded to *Scorpion*.

USS *Grayback* (SS-208)

Grayback was launched on 31 January 1941 by Mrs Wilson Brown, wife of Rear-Admiral Brown who was Superintendent of the Naval Academy. The ceremony took place at the Electric Boat Company's yard at Groton, Connecticut and the submarine was commissioned on 30 June 1941 with Lt-Cmdr Willard A. Saunders in command.

After shakedown *Grayback*, and her sister USS *Grampus* (SS-207), headed for the Caribbean to take part in a modified war patrol, returning to Portsmouth, New Hampshire, on 30 November. After America's entry into the war she sailed from Portsmouth on 12 January 1942 arriving at Pearl on 8 February.

Grayback's first war patrol began on 15 February with orders to patrol the areas of Saipan and Guam. It was in that area that she played a deadly game of tag with a Japanese I-class submarine and it was four days before they lost contact. On 17 March came her first victory when she sank the 3,291-ton ex-collier *Ishikari Maru*. The patrol ended on 10 April.

The launching of *Grayback* at Groton on 31 January 1941.

Her second patrol was uneventful and she arrived at her new base of Fremantle, Australia, on 22 June 1942.

Grayback's third patrol was equally uneventful, although on the fourth she claimed to have hit a number of enemy ships, but none were confirmed apart from damaging the 7,191-ton transport *Noto Maru* in the Rabaul area. This attack was made by Lt-Cmdr Edward C. Stephan who had assumed command at the start of the fourth patrol. The authorities were not pleased as Stephan had expended all of the Grayback's twenty-four torpedoes for one damaged vessel, but he was allowed to keep his command.

The fifth war patrol commenced on 7 December 1942 and just one week later, her Pharmacist's Mate Harry B. Roby had to operate on an appendicitis case. This was the second appendectomy to have been carried out aboard a submarine on patrol; the first had taken place aboard the USS *Seadragon* (SS-194).

Grayback's large conning tower and white numbers are prominent in this May 1941 photograph.

On 25 December *Grayback* gave the Japanese a Christmas present when she battle-surfaced to destroy four enemy landing barges with her deck gun. On 3 January 1943 she claimed to have sunk a Japanese submarine, reported as the I-18, in a night surface attack, but post-war Japanese records show that this boat was destroyed in a combined attack by a Kingfisher aircraft catapulted from the cruiser USS *Helena* (CL-50) and the destroyer USS *Fletcher* (DD-445) on 11 February 1943. The subject of *Grayback's* attack remains unknown. On 5 January she was directed to rescue aviators from a downed B-26 Marauder who had hidden out in the jungle on Munda Island. She sent two men ashore in a rubber boat to locate the fliers and then surfaced the following night to rescue the six airmen and collect their own two crew members. *Grayback* then continued on her patrol. On the 17th she received a heavy depth-charging from an enemy destroyer with nineteen well-placed explosions causing damage and a resulting leak forced her back to Brisbane where she arrived on 23 February.

Her sixth patrol was unsuccessful, but during the seventh things began to improve after leaving Brisbane on 25 April 1943. On 11 May she attacked a convoy sinking the 6,441-ton cargo ship *Yodogawa Maru* and damaging two others. On the 16th she badly damaged the destroyer *Yugure* with two torpedoes and two months later this vessel was sunk by the USAAF in the Vella Lavella Gulf. The 5,829-ton freighter *England Maru* was *Grayback's* victim on 17 May and she also damaged a cargo ship estimated at 6,000 tons. The submarine returned to Pearl Harbor on 30 May after her most successful patrol so far. She then headed for San Francisco for overhaul at Mare Island and during the refit she was one of the first boats to be fitted with a 5-inch gun.

Grayback had a new skipper, Commander John A. Moore, for her eighth patrol and she sailed from Pearl Harbor on 26 September in company with the USS *Cero* (SS-225) and USS *Shad* (SS-235). The three-submarine wolfpack was a great success as they returned from the China Sea with claims of 38,000 tons sunk and 63,300 tons damaged. *Grayback* herself despatched the 7,072-ton passenger/cargo *Kozui Maru* on 14 October and the former light cruiser *Awata Maru*, a vessel of 7,398 tons, on the 22nd. On the 27th she and *Shad* combined efforts to sink the 9,138-ton transport *Fuji Maru*. All the submarines returned safely to Midway on 10 November then on to Pearl.

Johnny Moore took *Grayback* out for her ninth patrol on 2 December and on the night of 18/19 December he sighted a four-ship convoy with three escorts. He sank the 5,588-ton cargo ship *Gyokurei Maru* with two torpedoes and then damaged a 4,000-ton freighter quickly followed by a 7,000 tonner. The destroyer *Numakaze* stayed behind the remainder as *Grayback* surfaced to chase them, but the enemy warship attacked the submarine from behind so Moore dived the boat and fired all four stern tubes literally blowing the *Numakaze* out of the water. On the 21st he sank the 2,627-ton passenger/cargo ship *Konan Maru* and the 515-ton ex-netlayer *Kashiwa Maru* and damaged two freighters, one 5,500 tons and the other 6,300 tons, for good measure. Having made fine use of all her torpedoes, *Grayback* headed for home. However, she was not finished because on 27 December the submarine battle-surfaced to sink a large fishing boat, estimated at 200 tons, with her new deck gun. She arrived back at Pearl Harbor on 4 January 1944.

Leaving Pearl on 28 January *Grayback* began her tenth war patrol; she called in at Midway departing from there on 3 February. On the 19th she torpedoed and sank two cargo ships, the 4,739-ton *Taikei Maru* and the 1,917-ton *Toshin Maru*. On 24 February *Grayback* sank the 10,033-ton tanker *Nampo Maru* and damaged the 16,975-ton transport *Asama Maru*. The latter vessel was sunk by the USS *Atule* (SS-403) on 1 November 1944.

On 25 February Moore radioed that he had only two torpedoes remaining and he was ordered to head for home. On the 27th *Grayback's* last two torpedoes sank the 4,905-ton freighter *Ceylon Maru* according to post-war Japanese records. The Japanese also reported that on the 26th a land-based Nakajima 'Kate' carrier attack-bomber detected a submarine on the surface and dropped two 250-kg bombs claiming one direct hit which sank the vessel immediately. One of these dates must have been erroneous for the only submarine which could have been in the area of the freighter and, later, the aircraft attack, was *Grayback*.

So ended the fighting career of a fine submarine, an aggressive commander and his seventy-nine gallant crew members who, in their last three patrols, sank nearly 46,000 tons of Japanese shipping — a shining example to other submarines operating in the Pacific.

Grayback received eight battle stars for her war service in addition to two Navy Unit citations.

The *Numakaze* was literally blown out of the water by *Grayback*.

Grayback's changed appearance after her overhaul in the summer of 1943.

Grayback accounted for 46,000 tons of Japanese shipping while under the command of Johnny Moore.

USS *Trout* (SS-202)

Trout was launched at Portsmouth Navy Yard on 21 May 1940 and was commissioned on 15 November under the captaincy of Lt-Cmdr Frank W. 'Mike' Fenno Jr.

She was on patrol to the northwest of Midway when the Japanese struck at Pearl Harbor and she later saw enemy ships firing on Midway, but after heading in their direction at full speed she was unable to catch them as they departed. The submarine then returned to her patrol area, but saw nothing after that. She entered Pearl Harbor on 20 December to witness the great devastation after the enemy attack.

Trout departed from Pearl on 12 January 1942 with ammunition for the US forces on Corregidor and after topping up her fuel tanks at Midway she headed for a rendezvous with PT-41 commanded by Lt John D. Bulkeley and this was made on 3 February. Bulkeley was later awarded the Congressional Medal of Honor for distinguished service in PT Boats. The torpedo-boat escorted the submarine into the South Dock where she unloaded her much-needed cargo. After unloading, *Trout* required ballast and Fenno was more than surprised when this turned out to be twenty tons of gold bars and silver coins which had been removed from banks in Manila. She then departed to continue her war patrol in the East China Sea. On the 9th she sank the 2,719-ton converted gunboat *Chuwa Maru* with two torpedoes and on 20 February sank a 200-ton patrol craft with one torpedo in a night surface attack. *Trout* arrived at Pearl on 3 March 1942 and her precious ballast was transferred to a cruiser, but Fenno had a major problem as one of the gold bars worth $14,500 had gone missing. A search of the boat found the bar in the galley being used as a paperweight, or so it was claimed!

On her third war patrol 'Mike' Fenno took *Trout* out of Pearl on 24 March and two weeks later arrived off the coast of Honshu after refuelling at Midway. On 9 April two small freighters were sighted heading towards Kobe, but she could not get into an attacking position. On the next morning *Trout* followed a smoke trail from an escorted steamer and Fenno fired two torpedoes which missed. The escort then gave her a hard time before the submarine was able to slip away.

On the 11th she put one torpedo into the 16,801-ton tanker *Nisshin Maru*, but the damaged vessel was able to evade two others. *Trout* was to tangle with this ship again some months later before it was finally sunk by the USS *Crevalle* (SS-291) on 6 May 1944. Two torpedoes badly damaged a 10,000-ton tanker on 24 April with the

Trout exercising shortly after her commissioning.

vessel heading for shore to beach itself to prevent sinking. The 6,521-ton freighter *Tachibana Maru* came to the aid of the tanker, but one torpedo from *Trout* made this vessel beach itself also. Four days later she sank a 1,000-ton patrol boat and on 2 May she sent the 5,014-ton freighter *Uzan Maru* to the bottom followed by the 2,119-ton *Kongosan Maru* on the 4th. She returned to Pearl on 17 May after a most successful patrol.

Such was the urgency of war at that time that *Trout* went right out again on 21 May and headed for Midway to join other submarines awaiting the expected Japanese attack. On 4 June she was attacked by a Japanese aircraft, but received no damage. Four days later she passed through a large oil slick and picked up two enemy sailors floating on a wooden hatch cover. The patrol ended at Pearl Harbor on the 14th.

A new commander was assigned to *Trout* for her fifth patrol and Lt-Cmdr Lawson P. Ramage took her out of Pearl on 27 August 1942. In her patrol area off Truk she was soon in action for on 10 September the submarine was detected by a patrol craft and she had to go deep for over ninety minutes while the Japanese vessel dropped forty-five depth-charges, but *Trout* evaded without damage. The converted net-tender, the 863-ton *Koei Maru* felt the sting of her torpedoes on 21 September and just one week later, on the 28th *Trout* badly damaged the 17,830-ton aircraft-carrier *Taiyo* with two hits out of a spread of five torpedoes and later received a heavy depth-charging from the carrier's escorts. The *Taiyo* had a similar brush with the USS *Cabrilla* (SS-288) almost a year later, before finally being sunk by the high-scoring USS *Rasher* (SS-269) on 18 August 1944.

Trout was badly damaged by a Japanese aircraft on 3 October 1942 as she was detected while at periscope depth. She was at 58 feet with the periscope being lowered when the first bomb hit. A second explosion occurred as the boat was passing 80 feet and both periscopes were badly damaged with prisms cracked and periscope tubes flooded. The patrol was terminated and *Trout* put in to Brisbane on the 13th.

With repairs completed she headed out for her sixth war patrol on 26 October and proceeded to the waters around the New Georgia Islands. She reported that she had fired a spread of five torpedoes at a battleship of the Kongo-class on 13 November but no hits were reported and it could have been that they failed to detonate. *Trout* returned to Brisbane at the end of the patrol on 23 November.

After a short refit *Trout* set out from Australia in 29 December to patrol an area off North Borneo. On 11 January 1943, with her seventh patrol well under way, she made contact with a large tanker and fired four torpedoes in a night surface attack. Two hit amidships, the third exploded prematurely and the fourth's progress was not known. Her target turned out to be the 17,549-ton tanker *Kyokuyo Maru* which, although badly damaged, was able to make it to safety. *Trout* destroyed two sampans by her deck gun on the 18th and on the 21st she thought she had sunk the 3,520-ton freighter *Eifuku Maru* as the submarine cleared the area as the enemy's stern was under the water, but somehow this Maru survived only to be sent to the bottom by the USS *Pampanito* (SS-383) on 7 February 1945. *Trout*, however, was credited with the sinking of an unknown cargo vessel estimated at 2,984 tons! Exactly two years earlier, 7 February 1943, *Trout* met up with her old enemy the tanker *Nisshin Maru*, but once again she was only able to claim damage with one torpedo. On the 14th she sank the 1,911-ton converted gunboat *Hirotama Maru* in a surface attack, with one torpedo being enough to send the enemy to the bottom. *Trout* completed her patrol and arrived in Fremantle on 25 February 1943.

Her first mission of the eighth war patrol was to lay mines in the Api Passage with 'Red' Ramage taking her out of Fremantle on 22 March. *En route, Trout* fired at a Japanese auxiliary on 4 April, but without results and, the following day, a similar action brought nothing. On the 7th she laid twenty-three Mk.12 mines exactly as planned and then patrolled the Singapore shipping routes destroying two large sampans with her deck gun on 23 April. No further action was seen and she ended the patrol at Fremantle on 3 May.

Lt-Cmdr Albert H. Clark took command of *Trout* for her ninth patrol which commenced 26 May. She was to perform special missions during this patrol landing six agents, $10,000 in cash and two tons of equipment on Basilan Island in the Philippines. On 12 June she landed a six-man army team under the command of Capt

J. A. Hammer, USA, and a large quantity of supplies and ammunition at Labangan in Mindanao. Three days later she sank the 3,000-ton tanker *Sanraku Maru* with three out of three torpedoes in a submerged daylight attack. She contacted three coastal vessels on 26 June and the 600-ton cargo ship and two 400-ton schooners were despatched by *Trout's* deck gun with some fine shooting by her gun crew. On 2 July she sent to the bottom the 2,866-ton *Isuzu Maru* with two torpedoes and seven days later she evacuated Lt-Cmdr Parsons, USNR, and four other officers from the south coast of Mindanao. The patrol terminated at Fremantle on the 20th.

Trout's tenth patrol took her to patrol the Surigao and the San Bernardino Straits after leaving her base on 12 August. Some thirteen days later she did battle with a large sampan and after stopping it, the submarine sent a boarding party to collect any papers, maps or other material that would be useful to US Intelligence. After taking five prisoners the vessel was sent to the bottom, with three of the Japanese later being released in a rubber boat off Tifore Island.

On 9 September it was widely reported that *Trout* sank the Japanese submarine *I-182*, but this was not possible as that boat had been destroyed by the USS *Wadsworth* (DD-516) south of Espiritu Santo in the Solomons on 1 September and this was confirmed in

One of the last photographs taken shows *Trout's* wartime modifications as she leaves Hunters Point.

post-war Japanese records. On 23 September *Trout* sank the 3,427-ton freighter *Yamashiro Maru* and the 3,483-ton transport *Ryotoku Maru*. She badly required an overhaul and she ended this patrol at Pearl Harbor on 4 October 1943 before heading for Hunter's Point, California.

With overhaul completed *Trout* returned to Pearl Harbor from where she departed on her eleventh war patrol on 8 February 1944. After calling at Midway for fuel she headed towards the East China Sea. Japanese records show that on 29 February 1944 one of their convoys was attacked by an American submarine with one vessel being damaged and the 7,126-ton passenger/cargo ship *Sakito Maru* being sunk. No word of this action came from *Trout*, but she was the only submarine in that area on that date and the loss was a mystery until the war's end. The records show that the Japanese destroyer *Asashimo* detected a submarine and after dropping nineteen depth-charges oil and debris came to the surface. The enemy vessel dropped a final depth-charge on the spot where the oil surfaced and no further contact was made.

The sea closed over the USS *Trout* forever as she, with her eighty-one brave crew members, went down fighting. She was awarded a Presidential Unit Citation for her second, third and fifth patrols and earned eleven battle stars.

USS *Tullibee* (SS-284)

Tullibee, last of the Gato-class boats, was launched at Mare Island Navy Yard on 11 November 1942 and commissioned on 15 February 1943 with Commander Charles F. Brindupke in command.

Crowds line the shore for *Tullibee's* launching at Mare Island.

After the usual trials and shakedown she arrived at Pearl Harbor's submarine base on 15 May 1943. Although eager to get into the war she did not depart on her first patrol until 19 July and while in the Caroline Islands area she made torpedo attacks on Japanese vessels on 28 July and 10 August, but without results. In the attack on the 10th she was rammed by an enemy ship which resulted in a bent No.1 periscope. On 14 August she missed again, but on the 22nd she was right on target when she sank the 4,164-ton passenger/cargo vessel *Kaisho Maru* and damaged a freighter estimated at 5,000 tons. *Tullibee's* first war patrol ended at Midway on 6 September.

Her second patrol began on 28 September when Brindupke headed the submarine for the assigned patrol area in the East China Sea. On 15 October *Tullibee* attacked a convoy, sinking the 5,866-ton transport *Chicago Maru* and damaging another of an estimated 8,000 tons, with one torpedo hitting the latter perfectly while two others exploded prematurely *en route* to the target. She claimed to have sunk a large tanker on the 25th, but post-war records failed to confirm this. On 5 November she surfaced at Okino erabu Island north of Okinawa and opened fire on an army barracks with her deck gun. *Tullibee* returned to Pearl Harbor at the end of the patrol on 16 November 1943.

The Marianas was the destination as *Tullibee* departed on her third patrol on 14 December, but this time she formed part of a wolf-pack with the USS *Halibut* (SS-232) and the USS *Haddock* (SS-231). Brindupke, as senior officer, took command of the pack and it was he who made the first attack when, on 2 January 1944 he fired four torpedoes at an I-class submarine in a surface attack, but the enemy was alert and evaded.

As a Japanese floatplane arrived *Tullibee* dived and as she went deep four bombs exploded close aboard, but caused no damage. On 28 January the three submarines rendezvoused at night and the skippers of *Halibut* (Galantin) and *Haddock* (Roach) came aboard *Tullibee* by rubber boat for a meeting to discuss tactics. This meeting was historic as it was the first time that a submarine commander had ever left his boat at sea during a war patrol. *Halibut* was low on fuel and tried to transfer some from *Tullibee* by hosepipe, but this was not successful. The wolf-pack then deployed and on the 31st *Tullibee* sank the 549-ton net tender *Hiro Maru* before returning to Pearl on 10 February. The wolf-pack had not been too great a success apart from *Haddock* heavily damaging the aircraft-carrier *Unyo* which was able to make it to Saipan. This vessel had a number of engagements with US submarines before she was finally sent to the bottom by the USS *Barb* (SS-220) on 16 September 1944.

Tullibee's fourth patrol was to take her to the area north of Palau and she left Pearl Harbor on 5 March 1944. Her assignment was to take part in 'Operation Desecrate' a carrier-air strike at Palau scheduled for 30 March. On the night of the 26th she sighted an enemy convoy consisting of three good-sized Marus and three escorting warships. Although the weather was squally *Tullibee* got into a good position and fired two torpedoes at the largest vessel from a range of 3,000 yards. About two minutes later a tremendous explosion rocked *Tullibee* throwing all the submarine's bridge party into the sea and the boat disappeared. However, back at Pearl Harbor none of this was known and *Tullibee* was reported 'Overdue and presumed lost'. On 29 July 1944 she was removed from the Navy list.

After the war's end, Gunner's Mate C. W. Kuykendall returned from a prisoner-of-war camp in Japan to tell of *Tullibee's* final battle as he was the only survivor. The submarine was the victim of one of her own torpedoes which made a circular run and sank the boat.

As the explosion occurred Kuykendall was hurled into the water and for about ten minutes he heard other voices in the night, but then all was silent. He kept on swimming until the following morning when he was sighted by a Japanese escort ship and he was used for target practice for a while before they decided to pick him up. Kuykendall suffered greatly at the hands of the Japanese with numerous interrogations before finally going to work in the Ashio copper mines.

It was a tragic end to the *Tullibee* and seventy-nine of her crew as a malfunctioning torpedo, this time, had done its job, but unfortunately not on the enemy. It was indeed fortunate that Kuykendall did survive or *Tullibee's* loss would have remained a mystery.

She was awarded three battle stars for her World War II service.

Tullibee heads out for Pearl Harbor in May 1943.

USS *Gudgeon* (SS-211)

On 25 January 1941 *Gudgeon* was launched at Mare Island Navy Yard, California, and commissioned on 21 April 1941 with Lt-Cmdr Elton W. 'Joe' Grenfell in command.

Her shakedown was conducted off the Californian coast and on 28 August she was ordered to sail north to Alaska. After a tour of possible bases in the area she departed for the warmer climate of Hawaii and she arrived at Pearl Harbor on 10 October. *Gudgeon* was on exercise when the Japanese attacked and proceeded immediately to base arriving at Pearl on 9 December. Two days later, in company with the USS *Plunger* (SS-179) she departed for the long voyage to Kyushu for her first war patrol.

Gudgeon became the first American submarine to sink an enemy warship when, on 27 January 1942, she sank the Japanese submarine *I-73* (it did not become *I-173* as widely reported, as *Gudgeon* had sunk it before the new numbering system was adopted on 20 May 1942). *Gudgeon* was returning to base with no enemy sinkings having been plagued by faulty torpedoes, when she was advised by Intelligence that an enemy submarine, which had taken part in the shelling of Midway, might cross her path. Sure enough the *I-73* was seen travelling on the surface at 15 knots 240 miles west of Midway and Joe Grenfell hit it with three torpedoes, which worked perfectly. *Gudgeon* returned to Pearl on 31 January.

After departing for her second patrol on 22 February *Gudgeon* was bombed by an SBD Dauntless dive-bomber from the USS *Enterprise* (CV-6) while the submarine was near Marcus Island. She had been running on the surface when lookouts saw the aircraft shaping up to attack and Grenfell ordered the boat under. *Gudgeon* was passing 80 feet when the bomb exploded, but luckily it did no harm. Other US submarines had received the same treatment and this added credence to the saying 'A submarine is nobody's friend'.

On 26 March she torpedoed and sank a 4,000-ton freighter and the following day she sent the 6,526-ton cargo ship *Nissho Maru* to the bottom southeast of Kumun Island. She entered Pearl Harbor at the end of the patrol on 15 April.

Gudgeon was due for overhaul, but such was the urgency of war that she was taken out of dry dock three weeks early and readied for sea in just forty hours. Departing Pearl Harbor on 18 May she was needed as part of the submarine screen off Midway and took part in one of the most momentous sea battles of the war. The

The brand new *Gudgeon* on her sea trials off the Californian coast.

submarine returned to base on 14 June 1942.

Gudgeon had a new skipper for her fourth patrol with Lt-Cmdr William S. Stovall, Jr, taking command. She departed 11 July and got into the action on 3 August when she sank the 4,853-ton freighter *Naniwa Maru* with two torpedoes. On the 17th *Gudgeon* damaged two large tankers northwest of Truk when she put three torpedoes into the 10,020-ton *Shinkoku Maru* and two into the similar-sized *Nichiei Maru*. The latter was sunk by the USS *Besugo* (SS-321) on 6 January 1945. *Gudgeon's* patrol ended at Fremantle on 2 September 1942.

She was now part of the Southwestern Pacific Submarine Force and William Shirley Stovall took her out again on 8 October for her fifth patrol. On the 21st she caught up with the 6,783-ton freighter *Choko Maru* south of Kavieng and sank it with two torpedoes. On 11 November *Gudgeon* made a daring attack on a seven-ship convoy, firing a spread of torpedoes at the overlapping ships and claiming a number of hits, but these could have been premature as the post-war investigation showed no vessel losses. Certain of great success in this attack she returned to Australia to celebrate on 1 December 1942.

Gudgeon's crew was able to spend Christmas in Australia before leaving for the sixth war patrol on 27 December. During this patrol no shipping was destroyed, but two important special missions were carried out when, on 14 January 1943, she landed six Filipino guerrillas and one ton of equipment near Catmon Point, Negros, and on 9 February the submarine evacuated twenty-eight men from the south coast of Timor. She returned on the 18th.

Lt-Cmdr William S. Post Jr took command of *Gudgeon* and she set out from Fremantle on 13 March. She did not have to wait too long before the action came when, on the 22nd, one torpedo was enough to sink the 5,434-ton freighter *Meigen Maru* and damaged another freighter estimated at 5,700 tons. On 24 March she badly damaged a 300-ton patrol craft with her deck gun. Five days later Post was right on target when the submarine sank the 9,987-ton tanker *Toho Maru* and eight hours later the 1,192-ton vessel *Kyoei Maru No.2* was damaged, but was able to escape only to be sunk by the USS *Dace* (SS-247) on 27 July 1944. *Gudgeon* ended the patrol on 6 April 1943.

Gudgeon was ordered to return to Pearl Harbor and left Fremantle on 15 April. *En route* she carried out her eighth war patrol and during this outing *Gudgeon* was, once again, to conduct a special mission. However, she was still on the lookout for targets and on 26 April she fired six torpedoes, in two attacks at a freighter estimated at 9,000 tons and Post believed they had damaged the vessel, but aggressive escorts stopped any confirmation. There was no mistake on the 28th when *Gudgeon* sent to the bottom the 17,526-ton liner *Kamakura Maru* which, it was reported, was to be converted to an escort carrier. Post attacked it on the surface at night and after firing four torpedoes he dived the boat, but as *Gudgeon* was going down her crew heard three solid hits.

Post took her back to periscope depth and readied more tubes for firing, but there was no need as the giant liner was going down stern first and soon disappeared. Even though morale in the boat was high, the hunting had to give way to the priority of the special mission and this took place on 30 April when the submarine landed four guerrillas and three tons of equipment near Pucio Point, Panay, in the Philippines. She evacuated three men at the same time. On 4 May *Gudgeon* battle-surfaced to destroy a trawler, estimated at 500 tons, with her deck gun. Survivors identified the vessel as the *Naku Maru*. The following day she claimed a 1,600-ton freighter sunk in another gun action and although she left it burning with decks awash, there is no record of the enemy vessel sinking. *Gudgeon* rounded off a fine patrol on the 12th when she sank the 5,861-ton freighter *Sumatra Maru* and then proceeded to her original destination, Pearl Harbor, arriving on 25 May 1943. She quickly left Pearl heading for Mare Island and a much needed overhaul.

Gudgeon was back in action on 1 September 1943 when she departed from Pearl Harbor for her ninth patrol and on the 17th she damaged a Japanese patrol craft with her deck gun, but withdrew as heavier units were sighted. Her next victim was the 3,158-ton freighter *Taian Maru* which she sank with two torpedoes on 28 September and the next day damaged the 3,266-ton cargo ship *Santo Maru*. This ship is believed to have been repaired and renamed *Sansei Maru*, but this made no difference as it was still despatched by a US submarine when the USS *Sawfish* (SS-276) sank her on 8 December 1943. *Gudgeon* returned to Midway on 6 October.

She proceeded to the China coast for her tenth war patrol which commenced on 31 October. At 0400 hours on 23 November she made contact with a four-ship convoy and in just over one hour *Gudgeon* had sunk the 6,783-ton transport *Nekka Maru* and the 870-ton frigate *Wakamiya* and badly damaged a 10,000-ton tanker and a 1,000-ton freighter.

Gudgeon in her final form in San Francisco Bay, 7 August 1943.

She tied up at Pearl's submarine base on 11 December with leave for the crew in Honolulu over Christmas being the next best thing to home.

Gudgeon's eleventh patrol was less successful with the only real action being on 11 February 1944 when she put two torpedoes into the *Satsuma Maru*, a freighter of some 3,091 tons which was already sinking due to an attack by China-based American aircraft. Although the submarine speeded up the sinking, she did not claim any credit for the vessel's destruction. *Gudgeon* returned to Pearl Harbor on 5 March 1944.

Bill Post reluctantly gave up command and five patrols and two Navy Crosses after joining *Gudgeon* he sadly bid farewell to her. He left for a much deserved rest and to take command of a new construction boat, the USS *Spot* (SS-413).

Gudgeon's new skipper was Lt-Cmdr Robert A. Bonin who came to her after being executive officer of the USS *Grayling* (SS-209). She sailed for her twelfth war patrol on 4 April 1944 and after topping-up with fuel at Johnston Island she departed from there on the 7th, but was never seen or heard from again. Japanese records show attacks on American submarines in *Gudgeon's* patrol area, first by aircraft on 18 April when Japanese aviators claimed hits on the bridge and bow of a submarine and on 12 May surface vessels depth-charged a US submarine off Saipan. Both these attacks could have been on *Gudgeon*, but no definite conclusion could be reached.

So ended the career of a fighting submarine with over 70,000 tons of enemy shipping confirmed as sunk. Sadly, her new commander did not get much of a chance to take *Gudgeon* to an even higher score, but her motto 'Find 'em, Chase 'em, Sink 'em' became the inspiration for all United States submarines.

Gudgeon received a Presidential Unit Citation for her first seven war patrols and was also awarded eleven battle stars.

USS *Herring* (SS-233)

Portsmouth Naval Shipyard launched *Herring* on 15 January 1942 and she was commissioned, with Lt-Cmdr Raymond W. Johnson in command, on 4 May 1942.

Herring was assigned to Submarine Squadron Fifty to operate out of Roseneath in Scotland, but she went directly to her first war patrol in the Mediterranean to take part in 'Operation Torch', the Allied landings in North Africa. She arrived on station on 5 November 1942 and soon opened her account on the 8th by sinking the 5,083-ton freighter *Ville de Havre*, a French vessel operated by

Portsmouth Navy Yard launched *Herring* on 15 January 1942.

Herring photographed in November 1943.

the pro-German Vichy Government. Her patrol ended at Roseneath on 25 November.

The second patrol commenced on 16 December 1942, but targets were hard to find and she returned to Scotland empty-handed on 29 January 1943.

Herring's third patrol was more successful as she claimed to have destroyed one of Hitler's menaces, a Nazi U-boat. She fired two torpedoes at the enemy submarine in a night surface attack on 21 March 1943 and it is assumed that *Herring's* victim was the *U-163*, commanded by Korvettenkapitan Kurt-Edward Englemann, a submarine with over 28,000 tons of Allied shipping to its credit.

The *Herring's* third, fourth and fifth patrols were under the command of Lt-Cmdr John Corbus, but the last two were devoid of action. The fifth patrol ended on 26 July 1943 in New London.

She was assigned to the Pacific and with her original skipper Lt-Cmdr Raymond W. Johnson at the helm she departed for her sixth war patrol. On 14 December she sank the 3,948-ton transport *Hakozaki Maru* and damaged a 7,000-ton tanker. She claimed to have put two torpedoes into a destroyer escort on New Year's Eve, but on New Year's Day 1944 she really celebrated by sinking the 6,071-ton transport and aircraft ferry *Nagoya Maru* and claimed a similar fate for a 6,000-ton freighter, although the latter vessel was never confirmed.

Herring's seventh patrol was under the command of Lt-Cmdr David J. Zabriskie Jr, and he claimed one torpedo hit on a destroyer on 23 March but that was the only near success that she had. Zabriskie was warned over this poor showing, but was given a second chance.

Herring topped up with fuel at Midway on 21 May 1944 and proceeded on her eighth patrol which was to be in the area of the Kurile Islands. On 31 May she rendezvoused with the USS *Barb* (SS-220) and after a conference of war the two boats separated with *Herring* soon making contact with the 860-ton frigate *Ishigaki* and the 1,590-ton vessel *Hokuyo Maru*, sending them both to a watery grave to the west of Matsuwa Island. On the morning of 1 June she sank the 3,124-ton transport *Iwaki Maru* and the 4,366-ton freighter *Hiburi Maru*, while they were both anchored at Matsuwa Island. A Japanese shore battery sighted a submarine on the surface and, after opening fire, two direct hits were made on the conning tower and the boat sank. A post-war investigation of enemy records reported that 'bubbles covered an area about five metres wide and heavy oil covering an area of approximately 15 miles'.

Zabriskie and his crew were lost on the boat's most successful patrol as he took his second chance, but paid the ultimate price. *Herring* was awarded five battle stars for her war service.

USS *Golet* (SS-361)

Launched on 1 August 1943 by Mrs Alexander Wiley, wife of Senator Wiley of Wisconsin, *Golet* slid sideways into the Manitowoc River in the usual way for the Manitowoc Shipbuilding Company of Wisconsin. Because of the narrow river, launching in the normal manner was not possible, so the company overcame the problem by launching the boats sideways with all twenty-eight submarines built there during World War II causing no problems. *Golet* was commissioned on 30 November 1943 with Lt-Cmdr James M. Clement in command.

Shipyard workers, VIPs and other guests gather for *Golet's* sideways launch at Manitowoc on 1 August 1943.

Golet is photographed during her sea trials.

After battle practice and various training exercises in the area around Hawaii, her commander was relieved and Lt-Cmdr Philip H. Ross took over. Ross was an experienced skipper who had successfully commanded the USS *Halibut* (SS-232) and with him as executive officer was Lt-Cmdr James S. Clark as prospective Commanding Officer. *Golet* departed Pearl Harbor on 18 March for her first patrol and headed for her patrol area around the Kurile Islands, Hokkaido's southern coast and eastern Honshu. Severe weather hampered all operations during the period that *Golet* was on patrol and she returned to Midway, with all her torpedoes, on 3 May.

Lt-Cmdr Clark assumed command of *Golet* and she set out from Midway on 28 May 1944 to proceed to the area off Northern Honshu for her second war patrol. She was never heard from again. A post-war search of Japanese records showed that an anti-submarine depth-charge attack took place in *Golet's* patrol area on 14 June 1944 producing oil, cork, rafts and other debris.

A message sent to her on 9 July was not acknowledged and she was reported as presumed lost on 26 July 1944. The eighty-two crew members perished without the great promise of this fine submarine ever being fulfilled.

Golet covered with ice during her trials in November 1943.

USS *S-28* (SS-133)

The *S-28* was launched on 20 September 1922 by the Bethlehem Shipbuilding Company of Quincy, Massachusetts. She was commissioned on 13 December 1923 with Lt Kemp C. Christian as her first commanding officer.

At the commencement of the war in the Pacific *S-28* was in Mare Island Navy Yard, California, having a complete overhaul. With the urgency of the time, the work was finished on 22 January 1942 and she sailed for her base at San Diego where the submarine returned to the Underwater Sound Training School. However, *S-28's* services were badly needed elsewhere and, with Lt-Cmdr John D. Crowley in command, she sailed north to operate in the Aleutians area. She completed five patrols from her base at Dutch Harbor, but the adverse weather made it hard for the old submarine and mechanical problems were many.

The *S-28* at Puget Sount Navy Yard on 24 June 1943 after undergoing a complete overhaul.

From 15 March 1943 she operated out of Esquimalt, British Columbia, Canada, to assist the Royal Canadian Navy in anti-submarine exercises. On 15 April she was ordered to proceed to the Puget Sound Navy Yard for overhaul. During the overhaul a number of modifications were made and new equipment installed.

With a new skipper, Lt-Cmdr Vincent A. Sisler Jr, she returned to Dutch Harbor and departed on her sixth war patrol on 13 July 1943. The S-28 patrolled the area off Paramushiro, but without success and on 16 August 1943 she returned to Massacre Bay, Attu, for a refit and solution to the problem of constant mechanical failures.

Her seventh patrol produced her first and only victory when on 20 September she sank the 1,368-ton converted gunboat *Katsura Maru* No.2 with two torpedoes after a game of cat and mouse when the Japanese vessel dropped depth-charges close to the S-28. She continued her patrol off the coast of Kamchatka, but on 10 October there was serious injury to a crew member immediately following by an appendicitis case and she returned to Attu on 13 October 1943.

The severe operating conditions took their toll of the *S-28* and she was ordered to proceed to Pearl Harbor arriving there on 16 November. After another overhaul she remained at Pearl operating on training exercises in Hawaiian waters.

On 3 July 1944, now under the command of a Naval reservist, Lt-Cmdr Jack G. Campbell, she left her base to commence an exercise with the Coast Guard cutter *Reliance* (WPC-150). The following day the S-28 submerged and was never seen again. All attempts to contact the submarine failed and on the 6th a large oil slick appeared in the area where the boat went down. The water in that area is 8,400 feet deep so no rescue or even salvage could ever be attempted.

A Court of Inquiry failed to establish the cause of the loss of the S-28 and her crew of fifty, but there was much regret that the submarine disappeared during a training exercise and not in a war zone which would have been a little easier to accept.

The S-28 received one battle star for her seventh patrol when the old warrior did get herself onto the score sheet.

USS *Robalo* (SS-273)

Robalo was a Manitowoc Shipbuilding Company boat and was launched broadside on 9 May 1943 and was commissioned under the command of Lt-Cmdr Stephen H. Ambruster.

After trials on Lake Michigan she travelled down the Mississippi River and then through the Gulf of Mexico and to the Panama Canal. *En route* to her assigned base at Fremantle *Robalo* carried out her first war patrol and on 13 February 1944 she fired four torpedoes at a cargo ship estimated at 6,200 tons. Although the submarine was at long range she claimed one hit, but Ambruster was not considered to be 'of suitable temperament' to be a submarine skipper and was relieved at the end of the patrol.

Robalo after launching at Manitowoc, 9 May 1943.

The new commander was Lt-Cmdr Manning M. Kimmel, a son of Admiral Kimmel who was forced to share the blame for the Pearl Harbor disaster. *Robalo* was assigned an area of the South China Sea for her second patrol with the main task being the destruction of enemy vessels that were resupplying the Japanese fleet at Tawi Tawi. The submarine made a number of attacks, without results, but on 24 April 1944 *Robalo* came close to destruction when a Japanese Mitsubishi G4M1 'Betty' bomber sighted the submarine and made an attack. As she was passing 55 feet one bomb exploded close aboard port side forward and at that time the main induction was inadvertently flooded by a personnel error, putting the boat out of control and she reached 350 feet before the descent was checked. There was a large amount of damage including some to both periscopes, the SJ surface-search radar was disabled and the JP sound head was also put out of action. Some repairs were able to be made and despite all these problems Kimmel remained on patrol. On 17 May *Robalo* claimed to have sunk a tanker of some 7,500 tons in a night surface attack, but the loss was not confirmed by the Japanese in the post-war assessment.

The submarine left Fremantle for her third war patrol on 22 June 1944 and set course for the South China Sea once again. After going through the Makassar and Balabac Straits she was scheduled to have arrived on station on 6 July. East of Borneo on 2 July she sent a contact report having sighted a Fuso-class battleship with two destroyers for escort and some air cover. No other messages were ever received and she was later presumed lost.

After travelling down the Mississippi River, *Robalo* heads towards the Panama Canal, 19 November 1943.

A note dropped from the window of a prison camp on Palawan Island in the Philippines eventually found its way to Dr Mendosa, guerrilla leader in the area. From its contents it was concluded that only four men survived a tremendous explosion probably caused by a mine on 26 July. The crew members swam ashore, but were captured by the Japanese and it was reported that these men were put aboard a destroyer which departed from Puerto Princessa on 15 August 1944. Nothing was ever heard from them again and how they disappeared remains a mystery. Was the destroyer sunk *en route* to its unknown destination or were they put to death? Thankfully they were able to get a message through which told of *Robalo's* fate, but it is sad that the four should have survived such a disaster only to lose their lives at some later date.

Robalo was removed from the Navy list on 16 September 1944 and was awarded two battle stars for her service.

USS *Flier* (SS-250)

Flier at Mare Island, 20 April 1943.

The Electric Boat Company launched *Flier* on 11 July 1943 and she was commissioned on 18 October 1943 with Cmdr John D. Crowley in command. Crowley joined *Flier* after five patrols on the *S-28*.

After departing from New London she arrived at Pearl Harbor on 20 December 1943, but not before she had a brush with a friendly merchant ship which fired thirteen shells at *Flier* before Crowley was able to escape in a rain squall. After preparing for her first patrol she sailed on 12 January 1944 and headed for Midway to top-up her tanks. She arrived on the 16th at the height of a storm and while attempting to enter harbour she ran aground on a reef.

The damage caused *Flier* to return to Mare Island, California, for repairs and she was not able to commence her first war patrol until 21 May. Her assigned area was off Luzon and on 4 June she made contact with a convoy of five merchantmen and, after chasing them on the surface, she dived to attack. Crowley was able to get between the columns of ships and fired three torpedoes each at two ships, but as he was about to fire the stern tubes he saw one of the enemy vessels turning towards the *Flier* in an attempt to ram. The submarine went deep and the convoy got away, but not all of them, as she sank the 10,380-ton transport *Hakusan Maru*. Post-war records also showed that a 4,000-ton freighter was damaged. On the 13th she attacked another convoy, but escort vessels bore in after *Flier* and she had to evade before she could observe any damage to the convoy. Large convoys seem to be dropping into Crowley's lap as, on the 22nd, *Flier* went after yet another convoy scoring four hits for six torpedoes fired, damaging the 4,000-ton freighter *Belgium Maru* and another of similar size. She continued stalking the same convoy and the following day put three torpedoes into a freighter estimated at 7,500 tons.

Flier arrived at Fremantle for a refit which was to be from 5 July

During the Mare Island overhaul the bridge received wartime modifications.

to 2 August 1944 when she departed for her second patrol to proceed to the coast off Indo China. The 13th was indeed unlucky for the submarine for while crossing the Balabac Strait on the surface *Flier* blew up with a tremendous explosion and went down in twenty to thirty seconds while still making 15 knots. Crowley and the other men on the bridge or in the conning tower were able to get off the submarine either by design or just good luck. At one time there were about fifteen men in the water, but only eight of them reached Mantangula Island after about fifteen hours of swimming. The survivors lived like castaways until 19 August when they made contact with some friendly natives who guided them to an Australian coast-watcher. He radioed to Australia and on the night of 30-31 August 1944 they were greeted by a wonderful sight as the USS *Redfin* (SS-272) skirted a Japanese ship anchored nearby to pick up Crowley and the other survivors.

It seems certain that *Flier* was yet another submarine lost by striking a mine and the introduction of FM sonar, mine-locating equipment later in the war no doubt prevented the destruction of other submarines. As it was, Crowley and his seven survivors mourned the loss of *Flier* and their seventy-eight friends.

Flier received one battle star for her World War II service.

Harder down the slipways at Groton, 19 August 1942.

USS *Harder* (SS-257)

Samuel David Dealey, a name which was to become synonymous with the *Harder*, for he was to be her only skipper and together they would add a great chapter to the history of submarine warfare.

Launched on 19 August 1942 by the Electric Boat Company at Groton, *Harder* was commissioned on 2 December 1942. After her shakedown off the East Coast she left New London to proceed to Pearl Harbor, but en route to Panama a US Navy patrol bomber attacked her forcing Commander Dealey to take the submarine down — fast! He then wrote in the boat's log, 'Whose side are these crazy aviators on?'

Harder's first patrol out of Pearl commenced on 7 June 1943 and she was assigned to patrol off Honshu, Japan. It was the shape of things to come when, on the 22nd she damaged the 1,189-ton tanker *Kyoei Maru*, then on the 23rd sank the 7,189-ton ex-seaplane tender *Sagaru Maru*. The following day she put one torpedo into a freighter estimated at 7,100 tons. On the 25th she claimed to have sunk a 4,400-ton freighter, but this was never confirmed. *Harder*, still on the prowl, approached a vessel which appeared to have stopped, but it was one of the submarine's previous victims which had been beached to prevent from sinking. Dealey decided to save his torpedoes and he put them to good effect as, on 29 June she sighted a small convoy and blew the bow off a 4,000-ton freighter, then put his last torpedo into a tanker of some 6,500 tons. It was during this patrol that *Harder* went deep to escape a beating from some escort vessels and, at over 300 feet, she hit the bottom burying her nose into the mud. Dealey joked that '*Harder* had made her first landing on the shores of Japan', but the joke nearly turned sour as it took 45 minutes to get her free! The first patrol ended at Midway on 7 July 1943.

After returning to Pearl Harbor for rest and recuperation *Harder's* crew were eager to make up where they had left off and she departed from Pearl Harbor on 24 August 1943. Once again, after calling in at Midway, she headed for the Japanese coast. While off Honshu on 9 September she sank the 3,010-ton freighter *Koyo Maru* and two days later the submarine despatched the 1,050-ton *Yoko Maru* with one hit from a spread of three torpedoes. Two more escorted freighters came into view on the 13th, but *Harder* was forced deep by the escorts after being spotted by a patrolling enemy aircraft and it was two days and many depth-charges later before she evaded her attackers. After a much-needed battery charge

Dealey was on the hunt again and on 19 September *Harder* sent the 814-ton freighter *Kachisan Maru* to a watery grave. Four days later the submarine sank the 5,957-ton tanker *Daishin Maru* quickly followed by the 4,520-ton cargo ship *Kowa Maru* off Nagoya Bay. On her way home she damaged a 200-ton patrol boat with her deck gun and, via Midway, *Harder* arrived a Pearl Harbor on 8 October 1943.

For her third patrol, departing on the 30th she joined the USS *Pargo* (SS-264) and USS *Snook* (SS-279) to form a wolfpack, but communications between the boats were poor and the planned joint attacks were never carried out. On 12 November *Harder* sank a 4,000-ton freighter which, at the same time, was being lined up for attack by Lt-Cmdr Ian C. Eddy in *Pargo* who was amazed to see the Japanese vessel blow up while he was taking aim! Strangely, this vessel was never credited to *Harder*. Later in the day Dealey took *Harder* to the surface for her gun crew to destroy the 460-ton patrol craft *Ch.20*. Three good-size transports came in for punishment on the 19th when *Harder* sank the 5,385-ton *Hokko Maru*, the 3,936-ton *Udo Maru* and, after midnight, the 5,949-ton *Nikko Maru*. She completed the patrol and arrived at Pearl on 30 November.

Harder, in common with other submarines fitted with H.O.R. engines, experienced a lot of trouble and for most of this last patrol had number four engine broken down completely. These engines built by Hoover-Owens-Rentschler caused so many problems that they had saved Japan 'about thirty or forty vessels' according to one US submarine skipper. *Harder* was ordered to Mare Island Navy Yard to be re-engined and did not return to Pearl Harbor until 27 February 1944.

She sailed for her fourth war patrol in company with the USS *Seahorse* (SS-304) on 16 March 1944 and proceeded to the western side of the Carolines to act as lifeguard for downed flyers. On 1 April the submarine made its famous rescue of a Navy Hellcat pilot from the enemy-held island of Woleai. With the injured flyer forced into the trees by Japanese snipers, Dealey put *Harder's* nose on a reef and held her in that position with skilful handling of her twin screws. Three crew members guided a rubber boat to the beach to pick up the aviator, but the line securing the raft to the submarine was parted by a Curtiss Seagull floatplane which had landed to assist in the rescue. Another volunteer jumped into the water and swam with a second line through the raging surf and, despite the constant sniper fire, all the crewmen and pilot, Ensign John R. Galvin, USS *Bunker Hill* (CV-17), arrived safely at the submarine. Circling overhead, Navy aircraft provided cover as *Harder* backed

After having new engines fitted, *Harder* leaves Mare Island on 19 February 1944.

away and headed for the open sea. It was a gallant rescue and excellent piece of seamanship by Dealey. On 13 April a Japanese aircraft sighted the submarine and obviously radioed her position for, soon afterwards, the destroyer *Ikazuchi* closed in for an attack, but at 900 yards Dealey fired four torpedoes. Just two were enough to despatch the 2,090-ton warship which sank in less than five minutes. A night periscope attack four days later sent the 7,061-ton freighter *Matsue Maru* to the bottom and one torpedo damaged an escorting destroyer.

On the way to Fremantle, *Harder* paid another call on Woleai on 20 April and, after surfacing during a rain squall, she fired on shore positions with the deck gun. The patrol terminated on 3 May 1944.

Harder left Fremantle on 26 May to commence her fifth war patrol with orders to patrol the area around Tawi Tawi. On the night of 6 June she entered the heavily-patrolled Sibutu Passage just south of Tawi Tawi and made contact with a convoy of three tankers and two destroyers. While on the surface *Harder* gave chase but one of the escorts detected her and turned to attack, however, once again, Dealey did not run. Holding position *Harder* launched three torpedoes and the 1,500-ton destroyer *Minatsuki* went down. The following day she sighted another destroyer searching for her, but the hunter became the hunted and three torpedoes slammed into the 2,520-ton *Hayanami* sending it to join the two others at the bottom. Dealey was not happy about orders to conduct special missions, but during the night of the 8th and 9th *Harder* evacuated six coast-watchers from the northern coast of British North Borneo.

One of the vessels sunk by the 'destroyer killer'. The *Hayanami* was despatched by *Harder* in the Sibutu Passage.

Later that day two destroyers were sighted and *Harder* submerged to attack, firing four torpedoes as the targets were overlapping. Two torpedoes hit the 2,033-ton *Tanikaze* which blew up and sank immediately and Dealey claimed a hit on the other vessel, but this was never confirmed by Japanese records. *Harder* was patrolling in her assigned area off Tawi Tawi on the 10th when Dealey sighted a large Japanese Task Force which included the giant battleships *Yamato* and *Musashi*. As the submarine manoeuvred for an attack an enemy aircraft spotted her while she was at periscope depth and one of the escorting destroyers rushed in for the kill. Dealey fired three torpedoes for a 'down the throat' shot and took *Harder* down deep, with the crew hearing two large explosions. Later the escorts and other aircraft pounded her with a prolonged depth-charge attack, but *Harder* was eventually able to escape with only minor damage.

Although the explosions were heard the post-war investigation showed no destroyer was lost at that time. Dealey wrote, 'Our fervent thanks go to the Electric Boat Company for building such a fine ship'. *Harder* was able to get off a contact report on the enemy force, but no US submarine was in a position to attack. With the bit between her teeth *Harder* called in at Darwin for more torpedoes and then went right out again to patrol the area south of the Celebes, but without further sightings. This action-packed patrol ended in Darwin on 3 July 1944.

Harder's 'destroyer killer' reputation spread quickly throughout the submarine force giving confidence to many submarine commanders and showing that they could dish out punishment rather than just having to take it.

Her sixth patrol was in company with the USS *Haddo* (SS-255) and USS *Hake* (SS-256) with the three sister ships departing from Fremantle on 5 August 1944. After calling in at Port Darwin on the 13th they headed for the South China Sea to patrol off Luzon and on the 21st *Harder* and *Haddo* joined other submarines to attack a convoy off Paluan Bay, Mindoro with the Japanese losing five freighters for a confirmed 32,410 tons. Early the next morning west of Manila, *Harder* sank the 870-ton frigate *Matsuwa* followed later by another, this time the 940-ton *Hiburi*. On 23 August 1944 *Harder*, *Hake* and *Haddo* were off Dasol Bay, Point Caiman, Luzon and on that day *Haddo* torpedoed and damaged the destroyer *Asakaze*

With her bow in soft sand, *Harder* goes close in to shore to rescue a naval aviator at Woleai. A Curtiss Seagull seaplane attempts to assist, but only got in the way!

which had been escorting the tanker *Nijo Maru*. While the damaged destroyer was being towed in to Dasol Bay it sank 20 miles from Cape Bolinao. The tanker then headed for Dasol Bay, but the Japanese patrol boat *No.102* (ex-USS *Stewart* (DD-224), captured by the Japanese at Surabaya in March 1942) and the escort vessel *CD-22* were alerted to assist it. However, the *Niyo Maru* arrived unharmed, but the enemy warships conducted a sweep of the area and the *CD-22* detected *Harder*.

It was reported that *Harder* fired three torpedoes at this vessel which took evasive action and then bore into attack with depth-charges. The USS *Hake* reported that she had sighted *Harder's* periscope, but then heard fifteen depth-charges in rapid succession coming from the same area. Japanese reports show that 'much oil, wood chips and cork floated in the neighbourhood of the attack'.

So Sam Dealey and his beloved *Harder* were gone delivering a bitter blow to the United States Submarine Force. He and his seventy-eight crew-members lie forever in the South China Sea, but the daring exploits of this submarine will never be forgotten.

Commander Dealey was posthumously awarded the Medal of Honor and *Harder* received a Presidential Unit Citation and six battle stars for its war service.

Sam Dealey, *Harder's* only captain, left behind an enviable record.

USS *Seawolf* (SS-197)

Seawolf was launched 15 August 1939 at Portsmouth Navy Yard, New Hampshire, and was commissioned on 1 December with Lt Frederick B. Warder in command..

As the war with Japan commenced *Seawolf* prepared for action and left Cavite for her first war patrol on 8 December 1941. She patrolled the San Bernardino Strait and on the 14th the submarine fired eight torpedoes at the seaplane tender *Sanyo Maru*, but missed although one was reported to have hit and failed to explode. *Seawolf* was then depth-charged by escort vessels, but without damage and she returned to Cavite on 26 December 1941.

There were no Christmas celebrations for her crew and on New Year's Eve she departed for Australia arriving at Port Darwin arrived on 9 January 1942.

By the 16th *Seawolf* was on her way again this time heading towards Manila Bay with over 30 tons of .50 calibre ammunition for the Americans fighting on Corregidor where she arrived on the 28th. *Seawolf* evacuated twenty-five aviators and spare parts, loaded up with torpedoes and then departed for Surabaya the following day.

Sailing from Surabaya on 15 February for her fourth patrol she proceeded to patrol the Java Sea paying special attention to the Lombok Strait area. On the 19th she attacked two freighters each estimated at 5,000 tons, but claimed only damage to both. She was in action again on the 25th, but after firing at two Marus at around 5,000 tons and also at a destroyer, no hits were confirmed. *Seawolf* fired at a cruiser on the last day of the month, but the one hit claimed was also not confirmed. Targets were coming along regularly, but Freddie Warder's luck seemed to be out; however, on 1 April he damaged the light cruiser *Naka* with one torpedo. The patrol ended in Fremantle on 7 April 1942.

After a much needed refit *Seawolf* set out from Fremantle on 12 May for her fifth patrol now assigned to the Philippine Islands area and made a number of attacks late in May and in early June, but for no results. On 15 June *Seawolf* got her first confirmed sinking when she put one torpedo into the 1,206-ton converted gunboat *Nampo Maru* off Corregidor. The submarine returned to her base at Fremantle on 2 July 1942.

Seawolf's sixth patrol commenced on 25 July and on 2 August she damaged a 7,000-ton tanker with one torpedo. On the 14th, Warder's aim was perfect when he sank the 3,113-ton passenger/cargo vessel *Hachigen Maru* and again on the 25th when the 1,349-ton freighter *Showa Maru* went to the bottom off Manila. On 15 September she returned to Fremantle.

Her seventh patrol took place between 7 October and 1 December and when success came it came quickly, as on 2 November *Seawolf* sank the 2,933-ton freighter *Gifu Maru* while the following day down went the 7,189-ton transport *Sagami Maru* off Davao Harbor. Five days later the submarine put two torpedoes into the 2,929-ton converted gunboat *Keiko Maru*, sinking the vessel immediately.

As the patrol ended *Seawolf* put into Pearl Harbor before heading towards the west coast for a complete overhaul. She arrived at Mare Island Navy Yard on 10 December 1942 and did not depart again until 24 February 1943 with a much changed appearance. 'Fearless Freddie' Warder had left *Seawolf* and her new skipper, Lt-Cmdr Royce L. Gross, took her out from Pearl Harbor for her eighth patrol on 3 April. She destroyed the 4,575-ton freighter *Kaihei Maru* on the 15th and the 389-ton auxiliary *Banshu Maru No.5* with one torpedo on the 19th. The following day the *Seawolf's* deck gun left a sampan, of about 100 tons, a blazing wreck. The old destroyer *Tade*, which had been converted to Patrol Boat 39, was her victim on 23 April in an attack 150 miles northeast of Formosa. Another Sampan was destroyed on the 26th and she then headed for Midway to complete the patrol.

The East China Sea was her destination as she departed for her ninth patrol on 17 May and on 6 June she was in action as she attacked a convoy firing a spread of torpedoes. One of these torpedoes hit a freighter, but failed to explode while another ran underneath a cargo ship and hit a destroyer damaging it. On the 20th *Seawolf* caught up with a four-ship convoy and ended the career of the 4,739-ton cargo vessel *Shojin Maru* and many of the Japanese soldiers it was carrying. She called in at Midway to terminate the patrol and then proceeded to Pearl on 12 July 1943.

The tenth war patrol was again in the East China Sea after leaving Pearl Harbor on 14 August and on the 31st she really got into the action after making contact with a six-ship convoy. *Seawolf* sank the 5,253-ton *Shoto Maru*, the 5,486-ton *Kokko Maru* and heavily damaged the torpedo-boat *Sagi*, but the latter survived only to be sunk by USS *Gunnel* (SS-253) on 8 November 1944. *Seawolf* continued to track the remains of the convoy and on 2 September put one torpedo into the 2,256-ton freighter *Fusei Maru* which refused to sink so Gross surfaced and finished off the enemy vessel with the deck gun. Three days later she destroyed two sampans with her gun. The patrol ended on 15 September.

Seawolf's eleventh outing took her to the South China Sea commencing 5 October. She added the *Wuhu Maru*, a 3,222-ton freighter to her score on the 29th and on 4 November the submarine sank the 3,177-ton passenger/cargo ship *Kaifuku Maru*. *Seawolf* damaged a 5,000-ton freighter on 9 November in a night surface attack. Gross took her into Pearl Harbor for a refit on the 27th.

With the refit complete she departed for her twelfth patrol on 22 December and proceeded to the East China Sea and really got into the action on the night of 10/11 January 1944. *Seawolf* tore into a seven-vessel convoy and sank the 7,523-ton freighter *Asuka Maru*, the 5,747-ton freighter *Yahiko Maru* and the 6,400-ton cargo ship *Getsuyo Maru*.

She also damaged another 4,000 tonner. On the 14th the submarine despatched the 3,651-ton freighter *Yamaksuru Maru* and damaged another on the following day. The patrol ended on 27 January 1944 with the sinkings later confirmed at a total of 23,361 tons.

Seawolf at the time of her commissioning.

Seawolf left Pearl two days later heading for Hunter's Point, San Francisco, for a major overhaul and did not leave the west coast to return to action until 16 May 1944.

Her thirteenth patrol commenced from Pearl on 4 June under a new commanding officer, Lt-Cmdr Richard B. Lynch, with the submarine's assignment being to make reconnaissance photographs of Peleliu in the Palaus to prepare for the forthcoming attack on that fortress. With the photography completed *Seawolf* patrolled the area from Peleliu to Yap and Ulithi. The patrol terminated on 7 July.

Another commanding officer arrived as 'Ozzie' Lynch left to take command of the USS *Skate* (SS-305); *Seawolf's* new skipper was Lt-Cmdr Albert M. Bontier. Al Bontier had commissioned the USS *Razorback* (SS-394) in April 1944, but unfortunately the new submarine ran aground off New London and after an investigation he was relieved of his command and assigned to *Seawolf*.

Her fourteenth war patrol started from Darwin and on 7 August she landed six men and ten tons of supplies at Tongehatan Point on Tawi Tawi and two days later she had a similar operation at Pirata Head, Palawan. This special mission patrol ended in Brisbane.

Seawolf departed from Brisbane on 21 September 1944 and by the 29th she was off Manus in the Admiralty Islands. The submarine received a special mission assignment to carry seventeen US Army personnel and stores to Samar. On 3 October she and the USS *Narwhal* (SS-167) exchanged radar signals off Morotai and shortly afterwards a Japanese submarine, the *RO-41*, torpedoed and sank the USS *Shelton* (DE-407). The USS *Richard M. Rowell* (DE-403) stood

by the sinking vessel as the destroyer escorts were part of a 7th Fleet task group which included the escort carriers USS *Midway* (CVE-63), later renamed *St Lo*, and the USS *Fanshaw Bay* (CVE-70). The *Rowell* went on a search for the enemy submarine and was assisted by two Grumman TBM Avengers from the *Midway*. One of the aircraft sighted a diving submarine some distance away and dropped two bombs. The destroyer escort speeded to the position which had been pinpointed by the aircraft and where a dye marker had been dropped. *Rowell* made sound contact with a submarine and immediately made an attack despite the fact that this attack and that of the aircraft were both in complete disregard of an Allied submarine safety lane. The US vessel made six attacks including five with the forward-thrown 'hedgehogs', and although the destroyer escort heard the submarine sending signals they assumed that it was an enemy attempt to jam their sound equipment. Underwater explosions were heard and debris came to the surface. There is little doubt that the submarine sunk was *Seawolf* as all attempts to contact her failed. A post-war investigation of Japanese records show that their submarine *RO-41*, under the command of Lieutenant Shiizuka, returned safely to base without any counter-attack.

So *Seawolf*, her gallant crew and seventeen army colleagues were gone and it was tragic that the old warrior was lost to a mistake by Allied forces after so many battles against a ruthless enemy.

She was reported lost on 28 December 1944 and was awarded thirteen battle stars for her war service.

Photographed on 9 May 1944, *Seawolf* heads out from the west coast. Note the much modified superstructure.

USS *Darter* (SS-227)

The Electric Boat Company at Groton launched *Darter* on 6 June 1943 and she was commissioned on 7 September with Cmdr William S. Stovall Jr, as captain.

She departed from Pearl Harbor on 21 December 1943 with William Shirley Stovall taking her out for her first patrol with orders to patrol off Truk covering the shipping lanes to the south and west of the island. After some mechanical problems needing repairs, *Darter* went back on patrol and on 13 February 1944 she damaged a cargo ship estimated at 7,500 tons. The submarine then received a heavy depth-charging from escort vessels before she was able to slip away. She then carried out lifeguard duty off Truk until she headed for Brisbane, arriving there on 29 February to end the patrol.

Darter completed a refit before leaving Brisbane on 17 March for her second war patrol which was to take her to the areas north of Western New Guinea and south of Davao. She topped-up with fuel at Milne Bay on 21 March 1944 and left on the following morning. She got her first confirmed victim on the 30th when she sank the 2,829-ton cargo vessel *Fujikawa Maru* with four torpedoes. In company with USS *Dace* (SS-247) she patrolled near Davao Gulf and on 6 April they made contact with an enemy force consisting of three heavy cruisers escorted by four destroyers. *Dace* fired a spread at long range, but missed and *Darter* was too far behind to catch the speeding targets. She patrolled the New Guinea area during the Allied Landings then refuelled at Darwin on the 29th before leaving the next day to return to her patrol area. *Darter* ended the patrol at Manus on 23 May 1944.

A new skipper arrived in time to take *Darter* on her third patrol with Lt-Cmdr David H. McClintock in command. She left Manus on 21 June heading for the Mindanao and Halmahera areas.

McClintock was soon on the scoreboard as, on the 29th, he put two torpedoes into the 4,400-ton minelayer *Tsugaru* to send it to the bottom off Morotai Island. The rest of the patrol was uneventful and *Darter* returned to Brisbane on 8 August 1944.

After leaving for her fourth patrol which was to take her to the Celebes and South China Sea, *Darter* had to return to Darwin to make some minor repairs, before leaving on 10 September. She received a fuel top-up at Mios Woendi and pulled out of there on 1 October with her old partner *Dace* to scout the South China Sea before the invasion of Leyte. She scored two torpedo hits on a

The Electric Boat Company launched *Darter* at Groton.

tanker estimated at 10,000 tons, but records do not show any sinking. *Darter* and *Dace* made contact with a large Japanese force approaching the Palawan Passage on 20 October and immediately *Darter* sent a contact report with the location of the enemy group. Both submarines then went in to attack with other US submarines closing in to assist. Targets were plentiful and on the 23rd *Darter* sank the 12,200-ton heavy cruiser *Atago*, which was Admiral Kurita's flagship and also damaged the 13,160-ton cruiser *Takao* while *Dace* despatched the sister ship *Maya*. *Darter* then started tracking the damaged cruiser through the Palawan Passage, but because of the furious action in the previous days she had been unable to get a navigational fix and at five minutes past midnight on the 24th she ran aground on Bombay Shoal. The submarine had been making 17 knots on the surface and was firmly stuck and despite all effects throughout the day, she remained high and dry. McClintock reluctantly radio Lt-Cmdr Bladen D. Clagett in *Dace* to inform him of the situation and knowing that *Dace* would have to forgo attempts to finish off the *Takao*. The heavily damaged *Takao* sought refuge in Singapore Harbour, but never put to sea again as it was sank by British midget submarines on 30 July 1945 while still undergoing repairs from *Darter's* attack. With all papers and secret equipment destroyed the crew transferred from the stricken submarine to *Dace* by rubber boat with the operation taking over two and a half hours. Demolition charges were set and McClintock left his command taking a wardroom ashtray as a souvenir.

Dace was departing the area when the charges detonated, but the explosion did not destroy *Darter* and it was decided to torpedo her. Clagett fired four torpedoes, but these blew up on the reef. The deck gun then put twenty-one shells into the hulk doing a large amount of damage, but she was still substantially complete; however, a Japanese aircraft arrived on the scene and forced *Dace* into a fast withdrawal. The USS *Rock* (SS-274) was ordered to torpedo *Darter*, but once again the reef prevented this and it fell to the six-inch guns of the USS *Nautilus* (SS-168) to finish the job. After fifty-five hits the stranded submarine was still not destroyed although she was so badly damaged that a salvage attempt would not be worthwhile. The wreck of *Darter* remained on the reef for over twenty years.

Dace, with 165 officers and men on board, arrived at Fremantle on 6 November 1944 after practically running out of food. *Darter's* crew were transferred as a unit to commission the new submarine USS *Menhaden* (SS-377) to Manitowoc, but she arrived in the Pacific too late to see action.

Darter and *Dace* both received the Navy Unit Commendation for their daring action against the Japanese cruisers and *Darter* received four battle stars for her war service.

High and dry on the Bombay Shoal, *Darter* remained there for over 20 years despite all efforts to destroy her.

USS *Shark II* (SS-314)

The only known photograph of *Shark II* was taken at her launch.

The second *Shark* was launched by the Electric Boat Company on 17 October 1943 and commissioned under the captaincy of Cmdr Edward N. Blakely on 14 February 1944.

Shark II's first war patrol was out of Pearl Harbor on 16 May 1944 and after calling at Midway she became part of 'Blair's Blasters', a wolf-pack under the command of Captain Leon N. Blair. The 'Blasters' were formed with the USS *Pintado* (SS-387), USS *Pilotfish* (SS-386) and *Shark*, and the group left Midway on 21 May 1944. As part of this attack group she proceeded to the area west of the Marianas and on the morning of 2 June sank the 4,700-ton transport *Chiyo Maru* and also damaged a freighter of over 5,000 tons. Two days later *Shark* attacked a heavily escorted convoy and sent the 6,886-ton cargo ship *Katsukawa Maru* to the bottom with four perfectly placed torpedoes. She continued to track the convoy and on the 5th Blakely showed his excellent shooting qualities when he sank the 7,006-ton freighter *Takaoka Maru* and a similar vessel, the 3,080-ton *Tamahime Maru*, both with perfect three out of three torpedo hits. *Shark* completed the patrol at Midway on 17 June 1944.,

After a refit she sailed from Midway for her second patrol on 10 July and headed for her assigned patrol area off Volcano and Bonin Islands. On the 19th she claimed to have damaged a 4,300-ton cargo ship and on 1 August a similar attack on a freighter was also unconfirmed in the post-war assessments. *Shark* went to lifeguard duties off Iwo Jima to support air strikes from the ever-growing fleet of carriers and on the 4th she rescued two aviators from one of the USS *Lexington's* (CV-16) torpedo bombers, but with no further pick-ups she completed her duty on 19 August before arriving at Pearl Harbor on the 29th.

Her third and last war patrol commenced on 2 October when she departed from Saipan. Shark had left Pearl on 23 September and upon reaching Saipan, Blakely formed the wolf-pack 'Blakely's Behemoths' with the submarines USS *Blackfish* (SS-221) and the USS *Seadragon* (SS-194), assigned to operate in the area midway between Hainan and the western end of Bashi Channel. On 22 October she made contact with the convoy, but could not get into a good firing position and the enemy ships escaped. Two days later she radioed *Seadragon* to report that she had made contact with a lone freighter and was going to attack. That was the last message ever received from *Shark* and she was reported lost on 27 November 1944.

Japanese records show that on 24 October the destroyer *Harukaze* detected a submarine and dropped depth-charges, but contact was lost. Another contact was soon made and seventeen depth-charges were dropped with this attack being followed by 'bubbles, heavy oil, clothes and cork' coming to the surface.

Shark II, lost with all hands in Luzon Strait, received one battle star for her short career.

Skipper Ed Blakely proudly wears the Navy Cross awarded for *Shark II's* excellent first patrol.

USS *Tang* (SS-306)

24 October 1944 was a black day for the US submarine force, but its significance was not known until after the war when it was established that *Darter*, *Shark II* and the famous *Tang* were all lost on that date.

Tang was launched on 17 August 1943 at Mare Island Navy Yard, California, and commissioned on 15 October with Lt-Cmdr Richard H. O'Kane in command. O'Kane had earned the chance to skipper a new boat after serving as executive officer to 'Mush' Morton on *Wahoo* and, as events would show, the next few glorious months would take both he and *Tang* to the top of the tree.

She arrived at Pearl Harbor on 8 January 1944 after the voyage from the west coast and after the usual preparations she left for her first patrol on the 22nd. *Tang* patrolled in the Caroline and Mariana Islands areas and soon after midnight on 17 February she detected a convoy and closed in to attack, but alert escorts forced her to break off, receiving five depth-charges in the process. However, *Tang* returned to put three torpedoes into the 6,854-ton cargo ship *Gyoten Maru* and it sank by the stern. Records show that at the time the 5,184-ton tanker *Kuniei Maru* was sunk, but for some reason this vessel's loss was not attributed to *Tang*. At midnight on the 22nd she made a night surface attack on a three-ship convoy to the west of Saipan, sinking the 3,581-ton passenger/cargo ship *Fukuyama Maru* and an hour later she sent the 6,777-ton *Yamashimo Maru* to the bottom off Truk. Two days later she detected a tanker and a freighter escorted by a destroyer, but bad weather prevented the submarine from getting into a good firing position. Never one to give up, O'Kane tracked the enemy ships until nightfall and then sank the 2,424-ton freighter *Echizen Maru* which went down in four minutes. On the 25th *Tang* was on target again when she despatched the 1,790-ton tanker *Choko Maru* with three torpedoes. The next day O'Kane fired *Tang's* last four torpedoes at a zig-zagging freighter and, unusually, they all missed! With no torpedoes left the submarine returned to Midway.

The second patrol started on 16 March 1944 with orders to proceed to the areas around Davao Gulf, Palau and Truk. The submarine made a number of contacts with enemy ships, but was not in the right position to make an attack. O'Kane was not happy when *Tang* was assigned to lifeguard duty near Truk, but again she made a valuable contribution to the war effort by rescuing no less than twenty-two downed aviators. Besides their safe rescue, the

The new *Tang* on trials in San Francisco Bay.

flyers were overjoyed at finding that the submarine had orders to terminate the patrol at Pearl Harbor.

Tang's third war patrol ranks Number One in Navy records for the highest number of enemy vessels confirmed sunk in one patrol. The patrol commenced on 8 June 1944 with the submarine heading towards her assigned areas in the East China Sea and Yellow Sea. Midnight was *Tang's* favourite hunting hour for it was at that time on 24 June that she attacked a convoy of six Marus escorted by sixteen warships. It was a text book surface attack as *Tang* sank the 6,780-ton *Tamahoko Maru*, the 4,399-ton *Nasusan Maru*, the 3,175-ton *Tainan Maru* and the 1,937-ton *Kennichi Maru*. On the 30th she was patrolling the shipping lane to Kyushu when along came an unescorted cargo ship and *Tang* quickly despatched the 5,706-ton *Nikkin Maru*. The 878-ton tanker *Takatori Maru* and the 998-ton cargo ship *Taiun Maru No.2* were sent to the bottom on 1 July. Independence Day was celebrated by sinking the 6,886-ton freighter *Asukazan Maru* and, later in the day, the 6,932-ton *Yamaoka Maru* off the west coast of Korea. Early in the morning of the 6th *Tang's* crew went to battle stations when a cargo ship was sighted and down went the 1,469-ton *Dori Maru* which was sunk with her last two torpedoes. This magnificent patrol ended with ten enemy ships sunk and with the post-war assessment giving a total of 39,100 tons.

O'Kane got *Tang* under way on 31 July 1944 for her fourth war patrol with both skipper and crew eager to keep up the momentum. She was to patrol the waters off Honshu and on 10 August she fired a spread of three torpedoes at a tanker, but all missed. However, she got back into the groove next day when she

Tang returns to Pearl Harbor after her second patrol. On deck are the 22 aviators rescued by her from the waters around Truk.

sank the 3,328-ton cargo vessel *Roko Maru* with one torpedo hit, but could claim only damage to a second vessel as the escorts bore in to attack. A depth-charging followed for the next thirty-eight minutes, but *Tang* evaded and then returned to periscope depth to see the escorts picking up survivors. There was no sign of the damaged ship although its sinking was never confirmed. A patrol yacht was her next victim when *Tang's* deck gun reduced it to matchwood on 14 August and on the 22nd she sank a small freighter, the 116-ton *Nansatsu Maru No.2*, with one torpedo off Mikizaki. The next day the submarine got near enough to the 8,135-ton transport *Tsukushi Maru* to see its crew in their white uniforms lining the bridge and superstructure, but spoilt their ceremony by sending the enemy vessel to the bottom with two well-placed torpedo hits. She was south of Mikizaki again on the 25th to sink the 834-ton tanker *Nanko Maru No.8* and its escort, a 600-ton submarine chaser with her last torpedo. Another successful patrol was completed when *Tang* returned to Pearl Harbor on 1 September 1944.

After overhaul she departed from Pearl on 24 September for her fifth war patrol and after a call at Midway she left there on the 27th. The Formosa Strait was her assigned patrol area and on 10 October *Tang* was credited with sinking the 1,658-ton freighter *Joshu Go* and on the next day, the 711-ton *Oita Maru*. On the 23rd she made contact with a large convoy with many escorts and in a night surface attack *Tang* gallantly tore into them leaving a trail of sinking ships which Japanese records only show as the 1,920-ton *Wakatake Maru*, the 1,944-ton *Tatsuju Maru* and the 1,920-ton *Toun Maru*. The Japanese also lost the 1,339-ton *Kori Go*, but for some reason JANAC did not credit *Tang* with the sinking. The submarine slipped the escorts and left the scene at full speed. It was a brilliantly executed attack, but she was not through because on the 24th she attacked another convoy sinking the 7,024-ton tanker *Matsumoto Maru* and the 6,600-ton tanker *Kogen Maru* was also sunk.

Four more large vessels were claimed, but not allowed after the war. It was during this attack that *Tang* was tragically lost due to a circular run by her last torpedo. The weapon struck in the after torpedo room and she quickly sank by the stern in 180 feet of water. Just nine survivors including O'Kane were picked up by the Japanese and subjected to harsh treatment before spending the remainder of the war in prison camps.

None of the information on the last patrol was known until the war's end when the survivors were released from captivity and Japanese records assessed. There seem to have been many discrepancies in the enemy records and *Tang's* score, like that of many other submarines, suffered from their poor book-keeping. O'Kane and his survivors were convinced that her total tonnage sunk should have been over twice the amount credited to the boat.

Nevertheless, in just nine months *Tang* was credited with sinking twenty-four ships for a total of 93,824 tons and it was indeed a cruel twist of fate that deprived her of even greater glory. She and seventy-eight gallant crew-members lie forever at the bottom of the Formosa Strait.

Tang received two Presidential Unit Citations and four battle stars for her World War Two service. Richard O'Kane proudly received the nation's highest award, the Congressional Medal of Honor.

Dick O'Kane, *Tang's* famous commander, survived her tragic sinking and eventually retired in July 1957 as a Rear Admiral.

Escolar was the first submarine to be launched by the Cramp Shipbuilding Company in Philadelphia.

USS *Escolar* (SS-294)

Escolar was the first submarine launched by the Cramp Shipbuilding Company of Philadelphia as she slid down the slipway just before her sister ship USS *Dragonet* (SS-293) on 18 April 1943. However, because of production difficulties both were not commissioned until over a year later with *Escolar*, under the captaincy of Commander W. J. Millican being commissioned on 2 June 1944.

'Moke' Millican was an experienced skipper who had destroyed over 20,000 tons of Japanese shipping while commanding the USS *Thresher* (SS-200) and, after a period ashore, he was given a new-build boat, *Escolar*.

She left Pearl Harbor for her maiden patrol on 18 September 1944 and, after topping-up with fuel at Midway, she joined the USS *Croaker* (SS-246) and the USS *Perch II* (SS-313) to form the wolf-pack 'Millican's Marauders', named after the senior commander of the group. They departed Midway on the 23rd assigned to patrol the Yellow Sea and on 30 September *Escolar* sent a message to the other pack members that she had fought a gun action with a patrol boat. She was not damaged in this engagement, but gave no details as to the damage, if any, done to the Japanese vessel. Her last communication was to report her position to *Perch* on 17 October 1944 and attempts to contact her after that date were unsuccessful. She should have returned to Midway around 13 November, but she did not arrive.

Escolar's last message reported that she was heading for the Tsushima Strait, but as Japanese records do not report any anti-submarine activity in that area it must be assumed that she struck a mine. Like a number of other submarines, the true facts will never be known, but the loss of a popular commander, his crew and their new boat was a sad blow to the Submarine Force.

A rare photograph shows the new *Escolar* arriving at Pearl Harbor after the long voyage from the east coast of the United States.

The wartime censor has blanked out the number 218 on *Albacore's* bow in this shot of the launching.

USS *Albacore* (SS-218)

A chill wind blew over the slipway at Groton, Connecticut as the Electric Boat Company launched the Albacore on 17 February 1942. She was commissioned on 1 June 1942 under the command of Lt-Cmdr Richard C. Lake. *Albacore* departed from Pearl Harbor on 28 August and for her first war patrol she was assigned to patrol the area around Truk. On 13 September she damaged a freighter of approximately 8,000 tons, while on 1 October the submarine put two torpedoes into a 6,000-ton tanker also claiming damage. A 4,000-ton freighter came her way on the 10th but *Albacore* once again could only claim for damage to the vessel. On the previous day she had detected an enemy carrier with a cruiser and destroyer as escorts, but she was kept at bay and never got into a good firing position. The submarine then headed for Brisbane.

On her second patrol Albacore claimed to have sunk the 10,438-ton transport *Gokoku Maru* on 10 December as the submarine saw much floating debris in the area of the attack. However, the Japanese ship must have limped away as it was confirmed sunk by the USS *Barb* (SS-220) on 10 November 1944. *Albacore's* first confirmed sinking came on 18 December when she torpedoed and sank the 3,300-ton light cruiser *Tenryu* south of Madang.

She patrolled the Bismarck Archipelago on her third war patrol and on 20 February 1943 she sank a 750-ton frigate before turning her attentions to the 1,850-ton destroyer *Oshio* which the submarine sank with one torpedo-hit out of four fired.

Albacore's fourth patrol was to cover the north coast of New Guinea and although a number of enemy vessels were sighted, the results were poor. The submarine's fire-control party was blamed with only three hits out of eighteen torpedoes fired.

A new skipper was in command for *Albacore's* fifth patrol with Lt-Cmdr Oscar E. Hagberg replacing Lake. Poor shooting still plagued the submarine with fourteen torpedoes fired at two different convoys with only one hit on a 6,400-ton transport on 19 July to show for it. Two other convoys were sighted, but *Albacore* was unable to attack.

Albacore's sixth patrol was uneventful except for the sinking of the 2,627-ton ex-gunboat *Heijo Maru*, but on the seventh the submarine saw a lot of action, mostly the wrong kind! On 8 November 1943 Hagberg had sighted a convoy and was giving chase when she was bombed by a B-25 of the USAAF which chose to ignore the enemy ships and attack *Albacore*, but luckily damage was only slight. On the 10th the same thing happened, this time she was bombed by a B-24 Liberator of the Fifth Air Force which caught Albacore as she was submerging. As she was passing 60 feet the bombs exploded near the bow and main lighting and auxiliary power were temporarily lost. The engine induction outboard valve had gone under the surface before being fully closed and the induction was partially flooded. The *Albacore* went down to 450 feet before she could be stopped and for the next two and a half hours she oscillated to various depths before the crew was able to bring her under control. Despite the large amount of damage the submarine remained on patrol and on 25 November she sank the 4,704-ton cargo ship *Kenzan Maru* with two torpedo hits out of the spread of five. The Japanese cruiser *Agano* had been damaged by the USS *Scamp* (SS-277) and *Albacore* was ordered to finish it off, but as she approached she was detected by the escorting vessels, depth-charged for four hours and missed her chance. At the end of the patrol, Hagberg was relieved of command.

Commander James W. Blanchard was *Albacore's* new skipper and took her, once again, to the Bismarck Archipelago for her eighth war patrol. On 12 January 1944 the submarine sank the 2,629-ton ex-gunboat *Choko Maru* and also the vessel it was towing, the small motor gunboat *H4*. Two days later two of *Albacore's* torpedoes put an end to the 1,950-ton destroyer *Sazanami*.

After a much-needed overhaul at Mare Island Navy Yard, California, *Albacore* returned to action with her ninth patrol being operated west of the Marianas and in the Palau area. On 19 June 1944 she intercepted a Japanese task force, under the command of Admiral Ozawa, en route from Tawi Tawi and heading towards Saipan to engage American forces. Jim Blanchard was amazed to find himself in the middle of the Japanese carrier group and selecting a large carrier as the target he immediately had trouble with the TDC — Torpedo Data Computer. Not to be deterred, he fired the six bow torpedoes by judgement and then was forced to go deep as three destroyers came into attack the *Albacore*. As she sought protection below, her crew heard one solid torpedo hit and then a second, but after the war it was learned that the latter was caused by a Japanese aircraft flown by Lt. Sakio Komatsu diving into the torpedo to prevent it from hitting the carrier. The one good hit had damaged Ozawa's flagship, the 31,000-ton aircraft-carrier *Taiho* and caused little immediate concern. However, later that day aviation gasoline fumes had spread through the ship and the carrier exploded and sank. This was a devastating blow to the Japanese,

An overhaul at Mare Island in April 1944 saw the latest changes being incorporated into *Albacore* including a new bridge and 4-inch gun aft of the conning tower.

but there was more to come that day as the USS *Cavalla* (SS-244) under Commander Herman J. Kossler despatched the 30,000-ton carrier *Shokaku*, a veteran of the Pearl Harbor attack. Blanchard was upset at 'missing a golden opportunity' and reluctantly, *Albacore* went on lifeguard duty to cover the air strikes on Yap and Ulithi. On the 29th *Albacore* was again caught on the surface and strafed by an enemy fighter plane which put a number of holes into the superstructure. On 3 July she attacked an inter-island steamer destroying it with the deck gun, but when it was later found that the 900-ton *Taimei Maru* had women and children on board Blanchard and his crew were saddened by the attack. He picked up five survivors as prisoners and ordered a rubber boat with food and water to be launched for the remainder. *Albacore* called in at Admiralty Islands to hand over the prisoners then headed for

Majuro arriving on 15 July. It was later learned that *Taiho*, Japan's newest carrier, went down taking with it most of the ship's aircraft and 1,650 crew members.

Albacore's tenth war patrol was carried out around the southern coast of Shikoku, Japan, and on 5 September she sank the 880-ton cargo ship *Shingetsu Maru* to the north of Muroto Saki. On the 11th one torpedo was enough to sink the 170-ton submarine chaser *Ch.165*.

For her eleventh patrol *Albacore* was under the command of Lt-Cmdr Hugh R. Rimmer, leaving Pearl Harbor on 24 October. After a fuel stop at Midway she departed from there on the 28th heading for the northeast coast of Honshu and south of Hokkaido. She was never heard from again and was lost on 7 November after striking a mine while running submerged off Esan Misaki. The destruction of *Albacore* was witnessed by a Japanese patrol boat which reported a large underwater explosion followed by floating oil and debris.

Albacore received a Presidential Unit Citation for her second, third, eighth and ninth patrols and also nine battle stars for her war service.

In her final configuration, *Albacore* was photographed on 29 April 1944.

USS *Growler* (SS-215)

Growler and Gilmore: the two names became synonymous in the history of the US Submarine Service.

Growler was launched on 2 November 1941 by the Electric Boat Company at Groton and was commissioned on 20 March 1942 with Lt-Cmdr Howard W. Gilmore in command.

For her first patrol she was assigned to operate in the area of Dutch Harbor, Alaska, and departed from Pearl Harbor on 24 June 1942. *Growler* was soon in action when, on 5 July, she signalled her intentions to the Imperial Japanese Navy when she sank the 1,850-ton destroyer *Arare* and heavily damaged two others, the *Kasumi* and *Shiranui*, in Kiska Bay. The submarine then completed the patrol and arrived back at Pearl on the 17th.

Growler's second war patrol commenced on 5 August, when she proceeded to the area around Formosa arriving on station on the 21st. On 23 August she fired three torpedoes at a freighter estimated at 5,000 tons, but they failed to detonate and the enemy vessel escaped. Two days later the submarine again fired three torpedoes at a passenger/cargo vessel, but this time they missed and the escorts then gave *Growler* a good working over, dropping fifty-three depth-charges, but causing no serious damage. On the same day she made an attack on a convoy sinking the 2,904-ton ex-gunboat *Senyo Maru* with two torpedoes. Gilmore made a night periscope attack on 31 August and, with perfect shooting, sank the 5,866-ton cargo ship *Eifuku Maru* off Sankaku Island. *Growler* despatched the 10,360-ton supply ship *Kashino* on 4 September as quoted by enemy post-war records although, for some reason, the submarine was only allowed to claim 4,000 tons for the vessel. On the 4th she also sank a large sampan by gunfire. Three days later *Growler* fired two torpedoes at the 2,204-ton freighter *Taiku Maru*, but one hit was enough to send it to the bottom in just two minutes. The submarine arrived back at Pearl on 30 September 1942.

After a refit, which included the installation of a new surface radar and a 20mm gun, *Growler* headed to the Solomon Islands area for her third patrol. Hunting was poor as, although a number of enemy ships were sighted, she was never in a favourable position to make an attack. *Growler* was now to be based in Australia and ended the patrol in Brisbane on 10 December.

On New Year's Day 1943 she departed for her fourth war patrol with orders to operate in the area between the Gilberts and Palau with special attention being paid to one of the Japanese main convoy routes through the Steffen Strait. The 5,857-ton passenger/cargo ship *Chifuku Maru* was sunk with two perfect torpedo hits on 16 January. On the 30th *Growler* made contact with a large convoy and was able to damage a freighter with one hit, but the escorts were alert and forced her deep making her break off the attack. A gunboat was sighted in the early morning of 7 February but this turned out to be the new supply ship *Hayasaki*, a vessel of some 950 tons. As *Growler* made a surface approach, the enemy ship spotted the submarine and turned to ram, taking *Growler's* bridge personnel by surprise. The distance between the ships was now too short for the torpedoes to arm and Gilmore ordered, 'left full rudder' and sounded the collision alarm. It was too late as *Growler*, making a good 17 knots, hit the enemy vessel full amidships. The Japanese then sprayed the submarine's bridge with machine-gun fire killing two and wounding other Americans including Howard Gilmore who ordered 'Clear the bridge!' As this was being carried out, Gilmore was hit again and knowing that he could not make it to the hatch he gave the immortal command, 'Take her down'. The crew hesitated, but it was obvious that Gilmore was not following and *Growler's* executive officer, Lt-Cmdr Arnold F. Schade, carried out the commanding officer's orders. For his heroic devotion to duty, sacrificing himself to save his ship and its crew, Gilmore was awarded the Congressional Medal of Honor.

Meanwhile, Schade had a badly damaged submarine to control as the collision had bent 18 feet of *Growler's* bow 90 degrees to port and bullet holes in the conning tower were pouring water into the boat. By skilful handling *Growler* limped into Brisbane on 17 February. A complete new bow was grafted onto the submarine and the opportunity was taken to make other changes including the cutting down of her forward fairwater with the addition of a new 20mm gun. The deck gun was moved forward and another 20mm mount was put in its place. *Growler* was ready for action again by 5 May 1943.

Lt-Cmdr Schade was rewarded by being given command of *Growler*, but her next three war patrols were relatively uneventful apart from an attack during the fifth patrol when she sank the 5,196-ton passenger/cargo ship *Miyandono Maru* and damaged a freighter estimated at 7,400 tons on 19 June. The seventh patrol proved to be full of mechanical problems and only eleven days after leaving Brisbane she was ordered to Pearl Harbor, arriving on 7 November. The submarine was then instructed to proceed to Hunters Point, San Francisco, for a complete overhaul.

Growler returned to action and left Pearl Harbor on 21 February

Growler in the original Gato-Class form off New London in February 1942.

1944, topping-up at Midway before heading off for her eighth patrol. This patrol was plagued by poor weather with heavy seas and a typhoon to contend with before she put into Majuro on 16 April to end the patrol. Schade then left for home before commissioning the new USS *Bugara* (SS-331).

For her ninth war patrol *Growler's* new commanding officer was Cmdr Thomas B. Oakley Jr, who took her out from Majuro on 14 May heading for the Luzon area. She formed a wolf-pack with the USS *Seahorse* (SS-304) and USS *Bang* (SS-385), but *Growler* was only able to sink the 1,920-ton transport *Katori Maru* and damage a large tanker; both attacks were on 29 June 1943.

Growler was lead submarine in another wolf-pack for her tenth patrol which commenced from Pearl Harbor on 11 August. 'Ben's Busters' named from Oakley's middle name Benjamin, consisted of the USS *Sealion* (SS-315) and USS *Pampanito* (SS-383) with their patrol area being in the Formosa Strait. In a night surface attack on an enemy convoy on the 31st, the three submarines created havoc with a number of sinkings claimed. On 12 September another convoy was sighted and the 'Busters' attacked again. This time *Growler* sank the 870-ton frigate *Hirado* (Japanese sources quote name as *Hirato* — a new vessel less than one year old) and the 1,950-ton destroyer *Shikinami*, while the pack members sank a number of other vessels. Unknown to the submariners the convoy carried British and Australian prisoners of war and it was not until three days later that, as the submarines passed through the area of the attack, they found men clinging to rafts and floating debris, but the voices they heard were English. It was quickly established that they were prisoners of war and, with other submarines being called in to assist, 159 Allied prisoners were rescued. The survivors were exhausted, but overjoyed at being safe and in the relative luxury of a submarine after their ordeal at the hands of the Japanese.

Ben Oakley led another wolf-pack, this time from Fremantle with the three submarines sailing on 20 October. It was *Growler's*

Repaired and overhauled after her famous encounter with a Japanese freighter, *Growler* was photographed on 5 May 1943.

eleventh patrol and she was accompanied by the USS *Hake* (SS-256) and USS *Hardhead* (SS-365). Early in the morning of 8 November *Growler* made contact with a small convoy and Oakley ordered the others to join the attack. *Hake* and *Hardhead* both reported that while the attack was taking place they heard what sounded like a torpedo explosion followed by a number of depth-charges. Whatever they were, *Growler* was never heard from again and although Japanese records show some anti-submarine activity at that time, no claims were made. Could the torpedo explosion have been yet another circular run? Nobody will ever know.

Although *Growler* was successful under both Schade and Oakley she will always be associated with Howard W. Gilmore and the highest traditions of the United States Submarine Service. She received eight battle stars for her war service.

Growler's last captain was Ben Oakley, seen here at Pearl Harbor. However, her name will always be synonymous with Congressional Medal of Honor winner Howard Gilmore.

USS *Scamp* (SS-277)

Scamp was launched by the Portsmouth Navy Yard, New Hampshire, on 20 July 1942 and commissioned on 18 September with Commander Walter G. Ebert as captain.

After the various trials and shakedown she headed for the Pacific and tied up at Pearl Harbor's submarine base on 13 February 1943. *Scamp* departed for her first war patrol on 1 March with a valuable cargo in the shape of Admiral Charles A. Lockwood, Commander Submarine Force, Pacific (Comsubpac) going along for the ride, but only as far as Midway as his superiors had forbidden him to go further. Having topped-up with fuel *Scamp* left on the 5th then proceeded to her patrol area off Honshu. She made her first attack on 16 March when she damaged a freighter of about 4,000 tons, but faulty magnetic detonators in the torpedoes caused much frustration with Wally Ebert ordering their deactivation. This seemed to work on 20 March 1943 *Scamp* damaged the 1,450-ton cargo vessel *Seinan Maru* and on the following morning she also damaged the 6,541-ton transport *Manju Maru*. The patrol ended at Pearl on 7 April 1943.

Scamp's second patrol commenced on 19 April taking her to the Bismarck Archipelago, but her only action was on 28 May when she damaged the 6,853-ton converted seaplane tender *Kamikawa Maru*. Ebert was determined not to let this vessel get away and early on the 29th he sent it to the bottom with two more torpedoes. With no further action she returned to Brisbane on 4 June 1943.

Scamp departed for her third patrol on 22 June patrolling off the Solomon Islands, but she had to wait until 27 July before any action came her way when, in the early hours she detected a convoy and picking out a large tanker she fired six torpedoes claiming hits before the aggressive escorts forced Ebert to take her deep. Her torpedoes had, indeed, struck home with two good hits on the 18,300-ton oiler *Kazahaya* which was a new vessel only just four months old.

The Japanese ship was able to survive this attack only to be sunk on 6 October 1943 by the combined attacks of the USS *Steelhead* (SS-280) and the USS *Tinosa* (SS-283).

In the afternoon of 27 July *Scamp* sighted a Japanese submarine which fired a torpedo at the American boat, but Ebert was too quick for the enemy as he took *Scamp* down allowing the torpedo to pass over. She was then brought to periscope depth and the firing party was right on the money when their spread of four torpedoes

An aerial view of *Scamp* as she leaves Hawaiian waters for the last time.

literally blew the enemy submarine right out of the water. The submarine was claimed to be the *I-24*, but it was not until the inspection of Japanese records after the war that this vessel was found to be the *I-168* which went down sixty miles off New Hanover. This was quite a scalp as it was the *I-168* that had sunk the carrier USS *Yorktown* at the Battle of Midway in June 1942. The *I-24* had been sunk northeast of Attu in Aleutians by the USS *PC-487* on 11 June 1943. The patrol terminated on 8 August 1943.

By 5 September *Scamp* was at sea for her fourth war patrol with her assigned area again being the Solomons. On the 18th she sighted a small convoy and damaged an escort vessel with one torpedo, but received minor damage herself after she was depth-charged. The 8,614-ton cargo ship *Kansai Maru* was sunk early the next day. She claimed to have sunk a freighter estimated at 6,000 tons on 21 September, but enemy records did not confirm this. The submarine's fourth outing ended at Brisbane on 1 October 1943.

There was no let-up as Ebert took *Scamp* out again on 22 October. Her fifth patrol was in the area from Truk to Kavieng and on 4 November she damaged a freighter with one torpedo. The 6,481-ton passenger/cargo vessel *Tokyo Maru* was hit by one torpedo on the 10th but the submarine was forced away by the escorts. Ebert later saw the ship being towed away, but records show that it went down while under tow. On 12 November *Scamp* put one torpedo into the 7,000-ton cruiser *Agano* damaging it enough for it to seek repairs at Truk where it stayed until 16 February 1944. However, soon after putting to sea it fell victim to the USS *Skate* (SS-305). *Scamp* suffered minor damage from two bombs dropped by a Japanese floatplane on 18 November 1943 and returned to Brisbane on the 26th.

The sixth war patrol lasted from 16 December until 6 February 1944 when she tied up at Milne Bay for a much needed refit. During this patrol *Scamp* stopped a lot of oil getting to the wrong people when, on 14 January, she sank the 9,974-ton tanker *Nippon Maru*.

Wally Ebert reluctantly left the boat he had commissioned as he was ordered to Burma to act as liaison officer to Navgroup China.

Scamp's new skipper was Cmdr John C. Hollingsworth who had served in the USS *Triton* (SS-201) before being ordered ashore to a desk job in San Francisco. He wished to return to action and was given *Scamp*.

Hollingsworth's first patrol in command and the submarine's seventh, commenced on 3 March 1944 with orders to operate in the convoy lanes between Mindanao, Palau and New Guinea. On 4 April she damaged a 200-ton trawler with her deck gun, but frequent gun jamming forced her to leave the enemy vessel as the preoccupation with its destruction left *Scamp* vulnerable while on the surface. On 7 April 1944, off Mindanao, Hollingsworth sighted

The Japanese submarine *I-68* before it was renumbered as *I-168* and which fell victim to *Scamp* on 27 July 1943.

a group of six cruisers escorted by destroyers and with extensive air cover, but before she could attack she was spotted by one of the aircraft. Taking her down fast, she was passing 40 feet when a bomb from a Japanese floatplane exploded close aboard resulting in severe damage. *Scamp* released fuel oil and air bubbles to convince the Japanese that she had been destroyed and this ploy worked as she was able to slip away. In the evening she surfaced to survey the damage and the crew were shocked to see just how much had been caused. The boat was listing to port at 17 degrees, while the rear decking was badly damaged with the outer hull being dished in, the port engine main induction was deformed and numerous other areas were damaged. Hollingsworth and his crew did a magnificent job to get *Scamp* in to Seeadler Harbor, Manus, on 16 April for repairs before limping to Pearl Harbor for an extensive overhaul.

She was laid up for nearly six months before being able to get into action once more when she left Pearl on 16 October for her eighth war patrol. After the usual fuel stop at Midway *Scamp* departed on 20 October heading for the Bonin Islands. Hollingsworth acknowledged a message on 9 November, but did not reply to a message transmitted on the 14th ordering *Scamp* to perform lifeguard duty off Tokyo Bay.

On 11 November a Japanese patrol aircraft bombed the source of a trail of oil left by a submerged submarine and a coastal defence vessel dropped seventy depth-charges in three runs in the area of the target. A large amount of oil and many bubbles came to the surface, but this time it was for real and *Scamp* was gone.

She was deleted from the Navy list on 28 April 1945 and received seven battle stars for her World War II service.

USS *Swordfish* (SS-193)

Mare Island Navy Yard, California, launched *Swordfish* on 1 April 1939 from one of the large slipways which were laid down to produce battleship-size vessels, but were idle until the war clouds gathered. She was commissioned on 22 July under the command of Lt Chester C. Smith.

At the time of the Japanese attack on Pearl Harbor, *Swordfish* was in Manila, but sailed for her first war patrol on 8 December 1941. Her patrol area was off Hainan, China, and she was soon in action putting one torpedo into the 2,728-ton cargo ship *Nikkoku Maru* on the 14th claiming it as sunk, but the vessel was reported to have run aground. The first confirmed sinking by a US submarine in World War II came on 16 December when *Swordfish* sank the 8,663-ton transport *Atsutasan Maru* south of Samah. On the 27th she had a vital mission to perform when she evacuated officers and men from Submarines Asiatic Command Staff in Manila and delivered them safely to Surabaya, Java, on 7 January 1942.

Chet Smith took *Swordfish* out for her second patrol on 16 January and proceeded to the Celebes. On the 24th two perfect torpedo hits sent the 4,124-ton cargo vessel *Myoken Maru* to the bottom near Kema, Celebes Islands, and on 14 February she damaged the 7,620-ton freighter *Amagisan Maru* off the coast of Davao. Another special mission was ordered for *Swordfish* on 20 February when she evacuated the President of the Philippines and his family from Mariveles, Luzon. President Quezon was landed at San Jose, Panay, two days later and then the submarine returned to Manila to take off other high ranking Filipinos. Her patrol ended at Fremantle, Australia, on 9 March 1942.

Her third patrol commenced on 1 April with orders to deliver forty tons of supplies to the gallant, but besieged fighters on Corregidor. *En route, Swordfish* learned that the Island had been overrun by the Japanese and she was instructed to patrol in the Ambon Island area. Hunting was poor and she returned to Fremantle on 1 May 1942.

Swordfish, now free of special mission status, departed for her fourth war patrol on 15 May and on the 23rd damaged a cargo ship claiming one torpedo hit on a 5,000-tonner. Smith was on target again on 29 May when, in the early hours, he put two torpedoes into the 1,946-ton cargo vessel *Tatsufuku Maru* sinking it in two minutes. This ship had been badly damaged on the previous evening by the USS *Seal* (SS-183), but managed to limp away only

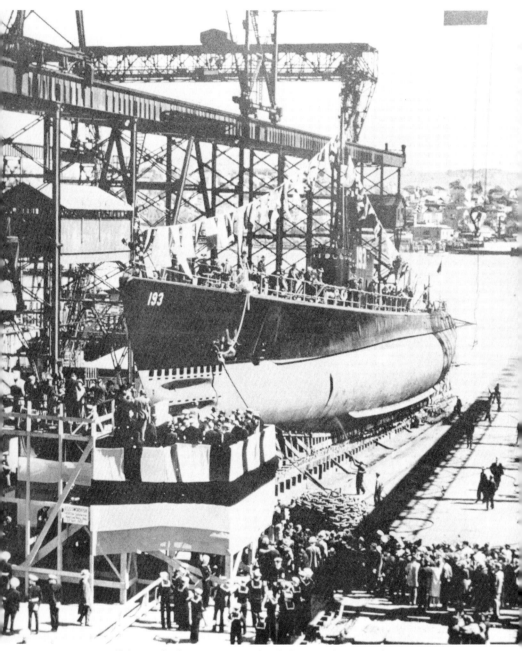

Swordfish was built on a Mare Island slipway designed for Battleship-size vessels, but was unused until the submarine contract was awarded.

to be caught by *Swordfish* four hours later. In the sinking assessment credit for the *Tatsufuku Maru* was given to *Seal*. No assessment was needed in June when *Swordfish* despatched the 4,585-ton freighter *Burma Maru* with two torpedoes in a night surface attack. She ended the patrol on 4 July 1942.

Near the end of the fourth patrol Smith caught a bad cold and command of the *Swordfish* was handed over to Lt-Cmdr Albert C. Burrows who took her out for her fifth war patrol. Chet Smith resumed the captaincy upon the submarine's return.

Her fifth patrol took the submarine to the Sulu Sea while her sixth was carried out in the area of the Solomon Islands, but neither of these patrols added any victims to the *Swordfish* scoreboard.

Lt-Cmdr Jack H. Lewis took command for her seventh patrol and on 19 January 1943 he destroyed the 4,122-ton freighter *Myoho Maru* off Bougainville. *Swordfish* was cruising on the surface approximately 150 miles north of New Ireland on 7 February, when a USAAF B-17 bomber roared in to attack at about 500 feet altitude. As the aeroplane's intentions were obviously not friendly, Lewis crash-dived the boat, but .50 calibre armour-piercing shells raked the bridge and superstructure, badly damaging the conning tower and some punctures occurred in the systems. The patrol had to be terminated due to the damage and *Swordfish* made it to Pearl Harbor on 23 February. After temporary repairs being made she headed for Mare Island Navy Yard, California, for a much needed overhaul.

Jack Lewis left *Swordfish* and headed for Philadelphia to take command of the USS *Dragonet* (SS-293) which was under construction at the Cramp Shipbuilding Company.

After the overhaul was completed she returned to Pearl and commenced her eighth war patrol on 29 July 1943 with Lt-Cmdr Frank M. Parker in command. On 22 August *Swordfish* caught up with the 3,016-ton cargo ship *Nishiyama Maru* and one torpedo hit was enough to send it to the bottom. She also claimed damage to a freighter estimated at 8,400 tons. The 3,203-ton cargo vessel *Tenkai Maru* was her next victim after attacking a convoy on 5 September. She arrived at her new base, Brisbane, on the 20th.

Yet another commander took over for *Swordfish's* ninth patrol and she now had Lt-Cmdr Frank L. Barrows in charge. However, the patrol only lasted for three weeks as mechanical problems plagued the submarine and defects were discovered almost daily. Barrows felt in some way responsible and after putting into Midway he asked to stand down as skipper of *Swordfish*. His request was granted, but as he was regarded as an able commander he returned to the United States to take a new construction boat, eventually commanding the USS *Moray* (SS-300).

Swordfish received a new commander in the shape of forty-two-year-old Captain Karl G. Hensel who was commander of Division 101 in Squadron Ten. Hensel was a tough taskmaster and a fine tactician who wanted to prove his theories in combat. He was thrilled at getting the old *Swordfish* and on 26 December 1943 she sailed for her tenth patrol, destination Tokyo Bay. Heavy weather hindered her progress and some of the old mechanical problems returned, however, Hensel was determined to make the patrol a success. In the evening of 13 January 1944 a convoy was sighted and *Swordfish* bore in to attack. Just after midnight she caught up with the 6,925-ton passenger/cargo *Yamakuni Maru* and sunk it with two torpedo hits.

Three enemy escorts then counter-attacked *Swordfish* dropping a total of twenty-four depth-charges that caused a large amount of, mainly minor, damage, but she was able to level off at 320 feet and escape her pursuers. The following day the submarine lost power in a dive and became uncontrollable, but after everything was blown she rocketed to the surface at the same steep angle as she went down. While on the surface with urgent repairs underway a Japanese patrol vessel was sighted and *Swordfish* just managed to regain power on one propeller and dive before the enemy spotted her. On the 16th *Swordfish* made three perfect torpedo hits on the 2,182-ton converted gunboat *Delhi Maru* which disappeared after a large explosion and Hensel was convinced that he had sunk an ammunition ship. Post-war records show that it was much more important as it was Japan's first Q-Ship equipped with concealed five-inch guns, depth-charges and the latest sonar and radar equipment. It was designed to lure unsuspecting American vessels, especially submarines, to attack before revealing the bristling armament. It never got the chance to trick anyone; *Swordfish* saw to that! The following day she received an Ultra Message to say that the Japanese carrier *Shokaku*, with four destroyers as escorts, was heading their way. Unfortunately, the sky was black and heavy rain made visibility poor, but radar picked up the enemy doing a good 27 knots. *Swordfish* submerged to periscope depth, but with the enemy group's speed they were on top of the submarine in no time and although Hensel and fired all four stern tubes, they all missed and the Japanese sped away. The enemy was probably not aware of the attack, but Hensel and his team felt bad about losing a carrier. *Shokaku* was eventually sunk by the USS *Cavalla* (SS-244) six months later. Morale on Swordfish improved as three torpedo hits sank the 3,140-ton converted salvage vessel *Kasagi Maru* on 27 January 1944. *Swordfish* arrived at Pearl Harbor on 7 February 1944 with Captain Hensel a very happy man as his one and only war patrol had been highly successful, earning him a Navy Cross and a lot of satisfaction.

Her new skipper was Cmdr Keats E. Montross who took the *Swordfish* to the Marianas area for her eleventh patrol after departing Pearl Harbor on 13 March 1944. On 5 April she damaged two cargo ships in a night surface attack in poor weather conditions, but no sinkings were ever confirmed. Without further action during this patrol the submarine put in to Majuro on the 29th.

The twelfth patrol was carried out in the area of the Bonin Islands and Montross got his first confirmed success on 9 June when two torpedoes relieved the Imperial Japanese Navy of the 1,270-ton destroyer *Matsukaze*. He was on target again in the early hours of the 15th when three torpedo hits sent the 4,804-ton cargo vessel *Kanseishi Maru* to the bottom. *Swordfish* was ordered to end the patrol at Pearl Harbor and she arrived there in the afternoon of 30 June 1944.

The old warrior was in need of a complete overhaul and did not put to sea again until leaving Pearl on 22 December. Nansei Shoto

Two torpedoes from *Swordfish* were enough to sink the Japanese destroyer *Matsukaze* on 9 June 1944.

was her destination for the thirteen patrol with an additional special assignment to photograph the beaches of Okinawa as part of the build-up to 'Operation Iceberg', the invasion of that heavily defended fortress. On 2 January 1945 *Swordfish* was advised to keep away from the Nansei Shotos as a series of large carrier air strikes were about to begin and she acknowledged the message on the 3rd. The submarine was ordered to continue the photographic mission in a message transmitted on 9 January, to which she was not required to reply. Another submarine, the USS *Kete* (SS-369) exchanged radar recognition signals with a vessel, which she believed to be *Swordfish*, on 12 January, but four hours later she heard heavy depth-charging in the area. Japanese records do not show an attack at that time, but they were sometimes incomplete and not always reliable. There was also a possibility that *Swordfish* could have run into some of the many mines sown in the Okinawa area and, perhaps, a chain reaction could have sounded like depth-charges to the distant *Kete*.

Whatever her fate the *Swordfish*, which had the first confirmed sinking of the war by a US submarine, was gone leaving behind a gallant fighting record and many heavy hearts throughout the US Navy. She received eight battle stars for her World War II service.

Swordfish as she appeared at the time of her loss.

USS *Barbel* (SS-316)

Despite extensive searching this photograph appears to be the only one existing of *Barbel*.

Barbel was launched by the Electric Boat Company on 14 November 1943 under the captaincy of Cmdr Robert A. Keating.

Her first war patrol commenced at Pearl Harbor on 15 July 1944 with a call at Midway on the 19th. The Bonin Islands were her assigned patrol area and she opened her account on 5 August by sinking the 970-ton cargo ship *Miyako Maru* in the Tokunoshima area. Two days later she claimed four torpedo hits on a large tanker, but post-war assessment failed to give credit. A convoy of three Marus and six escorts was attacked on the 9th with Keating sinking the 1,937-ton cargo ship *Yagi Maru* and a similar type of 2,330 tons, the *Boko Maru*. *Barbel's* aggressive first patrol ended at Majuro on 21 August.

The second patrol began as *Barbel* left Majuro on 13 September 1944 with orders to proceed to the Nansei Shotos. Late in the evening of the 25th she sank the 1,223-ton cargo ship *Bushu Maru*, damaged another estimated at 4,000 tons and also claimed to have sunk a destroyer escort. The 13th of October was unlucky for the Japanese as *Barbel* scored two torpedo hits on a destroyer and one on a tanker, before having to break off the action. She rendezvoused with the USS *Salmon* (SS-182) on 18 October to take off an officer who was dangerously ill and then delivered him safely to hospital in Saipan when the patrol terminated there on the 24th.

Barbel was soon at sea again as she departed for her third patrol on 30 October and headed for the area around the Philippines. A six-ship convoy was sighted on 14 November and she wasted no time in sinking the 4,422-ton transport *Misaki Maru* and continued to track the convoy until the following day when the submarine sank the 4,379-ton cargo vessel *Sugiyama Maru* with one well-placed torpedo. Ten days later she fired a spread of six torpedoes at a Japanese destroyer, but as they all missed through some excellent seamanship by the enemy captain, Keating decided to leave the area quickly! *Barbel* put into Fremantle at the end of the patrol on 7 December 1944.

A new skipper was awaiting *Barbel* as she arrived in Australia. Lt-Cmdr Conde L. Raguet was an up-and-coming young officer who had shown much potential when executive officer of the USS *Blackfin* (SS-322) and his reward was the command of *Barbel*.

The South China Sea was the destination for their fourth war patrol when she departed from Fremantle on 5 January 1945 and she proceeded to that area via the Lombok Strait, Java Sea and the Karimata Strait. On 3 February she reported that she had been attacked by Japanese aircraft on 31 January and 1 February and that she would transmit further information the next night. The USS *Tuna* (SS-203) was unable to contact *Barbel*, but had transmitted a message to her requesting a rendezvous on 7 February, but she never appeared. Enemy aviators reported to have successfully bombed a submarine on 4 February southwest of Palawan with one bomb landing near the bridge.

So perished *Barbel* with Raguet, at thirty years of age, being the youngest fleet boat commander to be lost in the war. She received three battle stars for her war service.

USS *Kete* (SS-369)

Manitowoc Shipbuilding Company of Wisconsin performed their usual sideways launching on *Kete* on 9 April 1944. The ceremony was performed by Mrs Edward S. Hutchinson, wife of the distinguished submariner and first commander of the USS *Rasher* (SS-269), another Manitowoc boat.

Kete's commissioning was on 31 July 1944 under Cmdr Royal L. Rutter, a veteran commander who had skippered the USS *Dolphin* (SS-169) until she was retired from active service.

Kete's maiden patrol commenced at Pearl Harbor on 31 October 1944 with her assigned area of operations being the East China Sea. She proceeded to the area in company with the USS *Sealion II* (SS-315), but extreme weather conditions and a problem with her bow planes forced her to put into Saipan on 24 November for repairs. It was not until a month later that *Kete* was able to resume the patrol and she departed with the USS *Kraken* (SS-370) to patrol to the

Kete hits the water in this fine launching shot at Manitowoc.

north of Okinawa. On 12 January she tried to make contact with another submarine which Rutter thought was the USS *Swordfish* (SS-193). Then she heard a barrage which could have been that boat's destruction. *Kete* arrived at Guam for refit on 30 January 1945.

Lt-Cmdr Edward Ackerman relieved Rutter as commander when the latter was ordered to Fifth Air Force Headquarters to co-ordinate submarine lifeguard activities.

Ackerman took *Kete* out of Guam on 1 March 1945 and sailed for the busy area around the Nansei Shotos. Besides the usual hunt for enemy shipping she was to gather weather information and perform lifeguard duties for the air strikes on Okinawa. On patrol west of Tokara gunto on the night of 9/10 March 1945 she sank three transports in a convoy, the 2,116-ton *Keizan Maru*, the 2,495-ton *Sanka Maru* and the 2,270-ton *Dokan Maru*. Then on the night of the 14th she unsuccessfully attacked a vessel she reported as a minelayer, but with only three torpedoes left she was ordered to Pearl Harbor for a refit with a call at Midway on the way.

Ackerman acknowledged this message on 19 March and on the 20th sent a weather report, but this was the last that was heard from *Kete* and, as she did not arrive at Midway as scheduled on 31 March, she was reported 'Overdue presumed lost'.

Kete's loss will always remain a mystery as no enemy action was reported. It could have been an operational loss, a mine explosion or an unreported enemy action. One theory is that she could have been sunk by a Japanese submarine which, in turn, was sunk before it was able to report any action. Four Japanese submarines were destroyed in that area and at about that time.

Kete was a new boat with a new skipper eager for success, but fate intervened and they lie forever in the deep waters between Okinawa and Midway Island. *Kete* received one battle star for her service.

Still awaiting her anti-aircraft guns and radar equipment, *Kete* was photographed on 15 August 1944 after her official commissioning date.

USS *Trigger* (SS-237)

Trigger was launched at Mare Island Navy Yard, California, on 22 October 1941 and was commissioned on 30 January under the command of Lt-Cmdr Jack H. Lewis.

Her first chance of action came when she departed from Midway in anticipation of the Japanese attack on the island. However, on 6 June 1942 disaster nearly struck as *Trigger* ran aground on a submerged coral reef and a tug boat was needed before she could be pulled clear. Her ballast tank was badly holed and the sonar heads had been knocked off, but although damaged, Lewis elected to keep to the mission. She returned to Pearl on the 9th.

It was 26 June 1942 before *Trigger* was ready for duty again and she sailed for the Aleutians, but after patrolling around Attu no attacks were made as, despite sighting a number of enemy vessels, the submarine was always out of position.

The famous *Trigger* is launched at Mare Island. Nobody at the ceremony could foresee the havoc that she would wreak on the Japanese.

Lt-Cmdr Roy S. Benson was *Trigger's* new commander as she departed from Pearl Harbor on 23 September for her second war patrol. Her assigned area was the waters around Japan and on 5 October an early morning attack with her deck gun went sour as the vessel turned out to be the 3,991-ton transport *Shinkoku Maru* which started to fight back with a vengeance. The Japanese ship then turned to attempt to ram *Trigger*, but Benson put two torpedoes into it to stop it in its tracks. Patrolling east of Hososhima on 17 October she sank the 5,869-ton transport *Holland Maru* in a surface attack in the early morning darkness. Later that day a destroyer came out of the Bungo suido and dropped a number of depth-charges near *Trigger*, but Benson then tried a 'down the throat' shot at the destroyer with a spread of three torpedoes. There was a tremendous explosion, but it appeared that there had been a premature detonation as the Japanese man-of-war was untouched.

Benson fired another torpedo as a parting gift, but this missed and the submarine cleared the area. A large tanker was claimed to be damaged on the 20th and just four days later another, the 10,526-ton *Nissho Maru* felt the sting of *Trigger's* torpedoes, but was able to limp away. The patrol ended at Pearl on 8 November 1942.

On 3 December 1942 *Trigger* left the friendly shores of Hawaii to commence her third patrol. The mission was to combine an offensive patrol with a minelaying operation and on the 20th she laid nineteen Mark 12 mines off Inubo Saki, just north of Tokyo Bay. On the 22nd Benson was perfectly placed to watch the 5,198-ton freighter *Teifuku Maru* enter the mined area and, seconds later, explode and sink. An escort circled the sinking vessel and later *Trigger's* crew heard another explosion and assumed that the warship had also hit a mine, but Japanese records do not confirm this. It was later found that the freighter had been loaded with aircraft so the cargo was more valuable than first thought. The New Year brought no joy for the Imperial Japanese Navy because on 10 January 1943 *Trigger* sank the 1,215-ton destroyer *Okikaze* 35 miles southeast of Yokosuka, with two well-placed torpedoes. *Trigger* returned to Pearl on 22 January 1943.

Roy Benson skilfully guided *Trigger* away from Pearl's submarine base on 9 February 1943 for her fourth war patrol which was to take her to the Palaus. On the 27th Benson fired four torpedoes at a large freighter but the captain was alert and was able to steer his ship between the torpedo tracks. The Japanese skipper then called for air support and the arrival of enemy aircraft made a second attack impossible. Heavy weather spoilt an attack on another freighter on

Trigger on sea trials soon after commissioning.

4 March, but on the 15th *Trigger* sank the 3,103-ton transport *Momoha Maru* and later that day she damaged the 5,854-ton *Florida Maru*. That night she fired six torpedoes at a freighter that was being towed by a smaller vessel. Five of the torpedoes missed the target, but the sixth made a circular run and passed over *Trigger's* engine room much too close for comfort.

A convoy was sighted on 20 March and she hit the 2,613-ton ex-gunboat *Choan Maru No.2*, but this vessel was able stay with the convoy even though it was heavily damaged. The patrol came to an end on 6 April 1943 after fifty-six days at sea.

The Japanese home waters were again *Trigger's* assigned patrol area after departing from Pearl Harbor on 30 April 1943 for her fifth outing. She was off Iro Saki on 28 May when she damaged the 975-ton tanker *Koshin Maru*. Benson was on target on 1 June when just one torpedo hit sank the 2,182-ton cargo ship *Noborikawa Maru*, but the real prize came along on the 10th when *Trigger* hit the jackpot — the new 26,949-ton aircraft carrier *Hiyo*. Two days earlier an Ultra message had alerted submarines in the vicinity of Tokyo Bay that two carriers were heading out and *Trigger* was the first to spot them. However, one of the submarine's engines was giving trouble and she could not get into a good firing position. Benson remained on station and after receiving another Ultra his patience paid off for out of Tokyo Bay came the *Hiyo* with an escorting destroyer on each side. The submarine made a perfect approach under one of the destroyers and fired all six bow tubes at the carrier. As *Trigger* went deep four explosions were heard and her crew was certain that the carrier would sink, but of the six torpedoes fired, one exploded prematurely, one hit but was a dud, two missed altogether and two hit solidly. *Trigger* returned to Pearl Harbor on 22 June reporting the probable sinking of a carrier, but the codebreakers knew differently. Apparently, *Hiyo* had limped back in to Tokyo Bay and after the war it was learnt that the carrier remained out of action until the end of September 1943. The Grim Reaper did catch up with *Hiyo* on 20 June 1944 when aircraft from the USS *Belleau Wood* (CVL-24) sank it 450 miles northwest of Yap.

After an overhaul, Trigger was like new and she had a new skipper to match in Lt-Cmdr Robert E. Dornin. On 1 September 'Dusty' Dornin took *Trigger* out for her sixth patrol heading for the East China Sea, operating north of Formosa. In the evening of the 17th she fired two torpedoes at a freighter and although both hit they failed to explode. Dornin continued to track the vessel and, next day, down went the 6,435-ton *Yowa Maru* after one good hit. Three days later she had a bonanza when she sighted a six-ship convoy and bore in sinking the oiler *Shiriya*, quoted by the Japanese Navy at 14,050 tons, but for some reason post-war JANAC assessment only allowed a credit of 6,500 tons! *Trigger* then sank the 7,498-ton tanker *Shoyo Maru* followed by the 6,662-ton freighter *Argun Maru*. In between these she had hit a tanker estimated at 7,300 tons and, on the stroke of midnight, the submarine badly damaged the 6,854-ton transport *Gyoku Maru*. This magnificent patrol ended at Midway on the 30th.

Trigger's seventh war patrol commenced on 22 October 1943 with orders to proceed to the East China and Yellow Seas. Two enemy transports were hit in an attack on 1 November, but two escorts closed in before she could confirm any sinking. Early the following morning Dornin sank the 7,148-ton transport *Delagoa Maru* and the 1,852-ton cargo ship *Yawata Maru*, each with three torpedo hits. *Trigger* was on target again on the 13th when she sighted a convoy of nine merchant ships escorted by four destroyers and, with her stern tubes, despatched the 4,443-ton transport *Nachisan Maru*. The angry escorts came in to attack the submarine, but only dropped five depth-charges while she was at 200 feet. However, these were enough to cause the No.2 main motor to vibrate and also caused a steady thumping sound in the reduction gear at depths below 150 feet and at all speeds. *Trigger* remained on patrol and on 21 November she relieved the Japanese of the 1,681-ton cargo ship *Eizan Maru* in the Yellow Sea before returning to Pearl Harbor on 8 December 1943.

There were no New Year's Day celebrations for *Trigger's* crew as she departed for her eighth patrol heading for the Truk-Guam shipping route. No contacts were made until 27 January 1944 when she sighted a Japanese RO-type submarine on the surface, but the enemy detected *Trigger* and turned towards her, so Dornin took no chances and went deep, cursing his luck. On the last day of January *Trigger* made contact with a convoy consisting of three ships escorted by two small warships and with two torpedoes sank the 11,933-ton submarine depot ship *Yasukuni Maru*. There were claims that the submarine had also sunk the small minelayer *Nasami*, but this was incorrect as Japanese records show this vessel to have been sunk by US aircraft at Rabaul when, after being damaged on 30 March, it went down on 1 April 1944. *Trigger* ended the patrol at Pearl on 23 February 1944.

Palau Islands were the destination for *Trigger's* ninth war patrol when she headed out on 23 March with Lt-Cmdr Frederick J. Harlfinger II in command. Early in the morning of 8 April 'Fritz' Harlfinger went in to attack one of the largest convoys ever seen by an American submarine with approximately twenty vessels escorted by twenty-five warships. After *Trigger* had fired four torpedoes she was detected and a destroyer raced in to counter-attack her forcing her to go deep. As they sought the depths, four solid hits were heard, but at that time their minds were

Her action-packed operations had taken their toll of *Trigger* as she arrives at Midway *en route* to Pearl Harbor after her ninth patrol.

concentrating on the enemy warships above. Six escorts eventually came after *Trigger* and she stayed down for seventeen hours, and was continually depth-charged which caused a great amount of damage. Rigged for silent running at 300 feet the temperature in the boat reached an incredible 135°F and it was decided to battle-surface to try and fight it out. However, at sunset the escorts relaxed and *Trigger* was able to evade their attentions. Making repairs while under way there were still some problems and on the 14th she rendezvoused with Dick O'Kane's *Tang* to borrow some spare parts for her air compressor. The *Trigger* remained on patrol and in the evening of 26 April she detected a six-ship convoy.

In the early hours of the 27th, Harlfinger went in to attack and with his overlapping shots scoring four good hits he claimed three freighters sunk. *Trigger* continued to track the convoy and the commander was convinced that the second attack sank two freighters and damaged another. The post-war assessment team only credited her with the 11,738-ton transport *Miike Maru* sunk and the 8,811-ton cargo ship Asosan Maru plus the brand new 870-ton frigate *Kasado* as damaged. *Trigger* put into Pearl on 20 May, but by the 24th she was on her way to Mare Island Navy Yard for a complete overhaul.

After returning to Pearl, she departed for her tenth patrol on 24 September 1944 with orders to perform lifeguard duty off the northeast coast of Formosa. Excitement came on 12 October when a burning Hellcat from the USS *Bunker Hill* (CV-17) ditched in the sea near to *Trigger* and the young pilot was soon rescued. With the invasion of the Philippines about to commence, *Trigger* sighted a Japanese battle group on 19 October. The enemy force consisted of five cruisers and several destroyers and, although she was too far out of position to attack, she did alert other forces to the threat. On the 30th *Trigger* damaged the 10,021-ton tanker *Takane Maru* and this was sunk by the USS *Salmon* (SS-182) four hours later. After damaging the tanker, the enemy escorts hounded *Trigger* dropping seventy-nine depth-charges, but no real damage was done. *Salmon* was also depth-charged and badly damaged and she radioed *Trigger* for assistance, which together with USS *Silversides* (SS-236) and USS *Sterlet* (SS-392), escorted the limping *Salmon* into the safety of Saipan arriving on 3 November. *Trigger*, in company with six other submarines, departed from Saipan on the 8th, but on the 17th she was ordered to curtail the patrol and head for Guam.

On 28 December 1944 *Trigger* began her eleventh patrol and proceeded to the Bungo suido and Kii suido areas. A Japanese submarine fired at her on 3 January 1945 and *Trigger*, not taking chances, cleared the area. On the 29th she made contact with a large convoy, but was too far away to catch up and attack. This patrol terminated at Guam on 3 February.

Now commanded by Cmdr David R. Connole, *Trigger's* twelfth war patrol commenced on 11 March 1945. Her patrol area was the Nansei Shoto sector and on the 18th Connole despatched the 1,012-ton cargo ship *Tsukushi Maru No.3* and damaged another estimated at 4,000 tons. She reported the attack on the 20th and was instructed to radio convoy movements and on the 26th she transmitted a weather report. On 4 April *Trigger* was ordered to proceed to Midway, but this message was not acknowledged and she never appeared at the island.

Post-war investigation showed that on 28 March 1945 a Japanese aircraft detected a submarine and bombed it. Surface vessels were guided to the spot and after two hours of intensive depth-charging a large pool of oil appeared. The investigation also showed that on the previous day a submarine had sunk the 1,564-ton repair ship *Odate* southwest of Ibusaki and this could only have been *Trigger*. So the gallant *Trigger* and her eighty-nine brave crew-members went down fighting.

In addition to the Presidential Unit Citation she received eleven battle stars for her war service.

Snook was launched at Portsmouth Navy Yard on 15 August 1942.

USS *Snook* (SS-279)

On 15 August 1942 *Snook* was launched at the Portsmouth Navy Yard, New Hampshire and was commissioned 24 October 1942 under the command of Lt-Cmdr Charles O. Triebel.

Snook's maiden patrol commenced 11 April 1943 when she pulled out of Pearl Harbor heading for the East China and Yellow Seas. Her first task was to plant twenty-four mines near Saddle Island off Shanghai and this was successfully completed on 30 April. In the afternoon of 5 May 'Chuck' Triebel sighted two freighters and tracked them until later that evening when conditions were favourable, then he calmly despatched the 1,268-ton *Kinko Maru* quickly followed by the 3,194-ton *Daifuku Maru*. Early in the morning of the 7th *Snook* was on target again and down went two more freighters, the 4,363-ton *Tosei Maru* and the 1,258-ton *Shinsei Maru No. 3*, but the latter was never confirmed. Before the patrol ended Triebel claimed to have sunk a 2,200-ton transport with one torpedo hit on 13 May and a 100-ton trawler by gunfire on the 16th. This aggressive patrol terminated at Midway on 23 May 1943.

The Ryukyu Islands were the destination as she departed for her second war patrol on 9 June. The submarine saw no action until the 24th when she heavily damaged the 7,986-ton tanker *Ose* west of Amami Oshima. *Snook* really celebrated the Fourth of July, as in the early morning she heavily damaged the 5,872-ton transport *Atlantic Maru*, but had better luck a little later when she sent to the bottom the 5,865-ton freighter *Liverpool Maru* and another, the 5,290-ton *Koki Maru*. After another successful patrol Snook put into Pearl on 18 July 1943.

She sailed from Pearl on 18 August 1943 to begin her third patrol with orders to perform lifeguard duty off Marcus Island during the carrier air strikes on 1 September. With no pick-ups made *Snook* took reconnaissance photographs of the island then continued on her normal patrol.

The 13th was unlucky for the 9,655-ton transport *Yamato Maru* as the submarine sunk it with one torpedo hit and on the 22nd she caught the *Katsurahama Maru*, a freighter of 715 tons, which went down off Dairen, China. Also on the 22nd *Snook* hit the small freighter *Hakutetsu Maru* with one torpedo, but this failed to detonate. She was heading back to Pearl when Triebel sighted a 300-ton trawler on 29 September and surfaced to sink the enemy vessel with the submarine's deck gun. The Japanese ship went down fighting and wounded four of *Snook's* crew before it eventually disappeared beneath the waves. She arrived back at Pearl Harbor on 8 October 1943.

The fourth patrol was in company with the USS *Harder* (SS-257) and USS *Pargo* (SS-264) with orders to patrol off the Marianas. On 28 November *Snook* shared with *Pargo* the damaging of a large cargo ship and then sank the 5,874-ton freighter *Kotobuki Maru*, but once again in the post-war assessment a submarine was not given credit for a vessel's destruction. Early next morning Triebel made no mistake when he sank the 4,928-ton passenger-cargo *Yamafuku Maru* and the 3,512-ton freighter *Shiganoura Maru*. *Snook* called in at Midway before heading toward Pearl Harbor where she tied up on 7 December 1943.

Kyushu was *Snook's* destination for her fifth patrol departing on 6 January 1944. On the 23rd she was in action off the Bonins when she sank the 3,120-ton converted gunboat *Magane Maru* and on 8 February *Snook* despatched the 6,989-ton transport *Lima Maru* with two torpedoes in a night periscope attack. She also badly damaged the freighter *Shiranesan Maru* in this attack, but this vessel did not survive for too long as it was sunk by the USS *Raton* (SS-270) on 18 October 1944. In a night surface attack on 14 February *Snook* sent the 3,591-ton cargo ship *Nittoku Maru* to the bottom off Tsushima and the following day it needed just one torpedo to sink the 875-ton freighter *Hoshi Maru No.2*.

The next vessel to feel *Snook's* sting was the 5,471-ton passenger/cargo *Koyo Maru* which went to a watery grave on 23 February. After the submarine ended the patrol on 6 March 1944 she was ordered to Hunter's Point, San Francisco, for a major overhaul.

'Chuck' Triebel had complained long and hard about the performance of American torpedoes and after five excellent patrols he was now relieved of command and ordered to the Bureau of Ordnance to assist in torpedo development.

With such a productive record *Snook's* new skipper had big boots to fill, but Lt-Cmdr George H. Browne was determined to take up where his predecessor had left off. However, the knives were out when, on her sixth war patrol, Browne fired at two freighters and missed on 12 July 1944 and for the first time *Snook* ended a patrol empty-handed when she put in to Midway on 14 August.

Browne was given the benefit of the doubt and he took *Snook* out for her seventh patrol to operate in the Luzon Strait area and the South China Sea. She had a mechanical problem and put in to Saipan for repairs on 25 September, but the repairs took longer than expected and *Snook* did not go to sea again until 4 October. Late in the evening of the 23rd, she detected a convoy and at midnight the 3,887-ton tanker *Kikusui Maru* went down after two torpedo hits. Two hours later Browne was on target once more when he sank the 6,886-ton cargo ship *Arisan Maru*, three hours after that, he sank the 5,863-ton cargo *Shinsei Maru No.1*. *Snook* rescued a Navy pilot from the sea on 3 November and arrived at Pearl Harbor on 18 November 1944.

Snook's eighth war patrol was also non-productive after patrolling off the Kuril Island where the only sightings of note were two Russian vessels and, luckily, she held her fire until their identity had been established. The patrol commenced on Christmas Day 1944 and ended on 17 February 1945.

Snook, under Cmdr John F. Walling was lost in April 1945 during her ninth patrol. She was operating in a wolf-pack led by the USS *Tigrone* (SS-419) and was assigned to lifeguard duties to the east of Formosa covering a British carrier strike. A Royal Navy Grumman Avenger from the fleet carrier HMS *Formidable* was forced down in *Snook's* area on 20 April, but messages requesting her to proceed to the crash scene were never acknowledged.

Nothing was ever heard from *Snook* again and her loss remains a mystery as no Japanese attacks were reported in that vicinity at that time. *Snook* received seven battle stars for her war service.

Snook's crew members wear their cold weather gear during her trials in January 1943.

Another fine view of a Manitowoc launching as *Lagarto* slides gracefully into the water.

USS *Lagarto* (SS-371)

Manitowoc Shipbuilding Company built *Lagarto*, launching her on 28 May 1944. She was commissioned on 14 October 1944 with the very experienced submarine Commander Frank D. Latta as skipper.

Lagarto sailed from Pearl Harbor on 7 February 1945 for her first war patrol in company with the USS *Haddock* (SS-231) and USS *Sennet* (SS-408). This pack was known as 'Latta's Lances', after *Lagarto's* commander and had orders to patrol the area around Nansei Shoto. The group sank three picket boats before *Lagarto* put an end to the career of the 880-ton cargo vessel *Taksumomo Maru* on the 24th. Also on that day she was given credit for the destruction of a Japanese submarine, but the identity has never been positively established with some sources quoting the *RO-49*, while others report it as the *I-371*. *Lagarto's* first patrol ended at Subic Bay on 20 March. The *RO-49* was claimed sunk by USS *Hudson* (DD 475) 60 miles west of Okinawa, 5 April 1945.

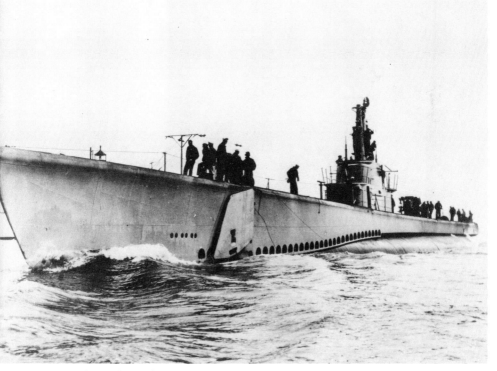

Lagarto during her trials.

Her second patrol began on 12 April and later that month she was ordered to patrol in the Gulf of Siam where she would be joined by the USS *Baya* (SS-318) on 2 May. The two submarines made contact and that night attacked a heavily escorted tanker, but the escorts were alert and kept the submarines at bay. On 4 May *Baya* tried to contact *Lagarto*, but without success and she was later presumed lost.

Japanese records show that that minelayer *Hatsutaka* attacked a submarine on 3 May and this could only have been *Lagarto*. The *Hatsutaka* did not celebrate for long as it was torpedoed and sunk by the USS *Hawkbill* (SS-366) on the 16th.

Lagarto went down with all hands and received just one battle star for her service in World War II.

A strange footnote to *Lagarto's* record came when she was awarded the sinking of the 5,819-ton cargo ship *Hokushin Maru* on 30 June 1945. This, of course, was not possible as the submarine had been lost almost eight weeks earlier!

USS *Bonefish* (SS-223)

Bonefish was launched 7 May 1943 by Mrs F. A. Daubin, wife of Rear-Admiral Daubin, at the Electric Boat Company's yard at Groton, Connecticut. The submarine was commissioned on the 31st, which must be a record time between the two events.

Her captain was Lt-Cmdr Thomas W. Hogan and he took *Bonefish* to her first operating base at Brisbane, Australia, where she arrived on 30 August 1943.

Bonefish was launched by the Electric Boat Company on 7 March 1943.

The submarine's maiden patrol was to take her to the Balabac Strait, topping-up at Darwin on 16 September before proceeding to her patrol area. After receiving some excellent Ultra messages Tom Hogan caught up with a fast convoy on the 27th and sank the lead ship, the 9,908-ton transport *Kashima Maru*, with two torpedoes. Two cargo ships were attacked on 6 October and, although hits were heard, no sinkings were ever confirmed. On the 10th two torpedoes each were enough to sink the 10,086-ton transport *Teibi Maru* and the 4,214-ton cargo vessel *Isuzugawa Maru*. *Bonefish* was ordered to end the patrol at Fremantle and *en route* she sank a good-sized schooner with her deck gun. The submarine put into Fremantle on 21 October 1943 and before breakfast the boat was visited by Admiral Ralph Christie to award Hogan the Navy Cross for a fine patrol.

Bonefish departed for her second patrol on 22 November entering the Flores Sea on the 28th. The following morning two of *Bonefish's* torpedoes sank the 4,645-ton cargo ship *Suez Maru* and it was 1 December when she was in action again sinking the 2,721-ton passenger/cargo *Nichiryo Maru* with one torpedo hit, then damaging an escorting destroyer before she was forced to break off the attack. A battle-surface on 11 December brought *Bonefish* into gun action with a minelayer estimated at 700 tons. She was able to damage the vessel before escorts forced her down with the resulting depth-charging only causing minor damage. The patrol ended at Fremantle on 19 December 1943.

After spending a pleasant Christmas and New Year in Australia *Bonefish* departed on 12 January 1944 for her third war patrol. She was to operate in an area off Indo-China and on the 22nd the submarine sank a large schooner by gunfire. Her bridge party and gun crew counted thirty-nine Japanese soldiers jumping into the water as the vessel went down. On 6 February *Bonefish* sighted a convoy and fired at two large vessels claiming hits on a tanker, thought to be a 19,000-tonner and a cargo ship estimated at 3,700 tons, but no information was ever forthcoming on this attack. Three days later Hogan fired at a large tanker and then had to go deep as a destroyer bore in to attack. The submarine's crew were convinced they heard three hits, actually it was four, but the massive vessel, the 19,262-ton *Tonan Maru No.2*, was able to limp away to safety. On the return to Australia, Hogan did not want to end the patrol as he still had thirteen torpedoes left aboard *Bonefish*, but stocks of food and fuel were low. He decided to put into Exmouth Gulf, replenish his supplies and head out once more, this time to patrol

Fremantle, Australia. *Bonefish* is the outer boat of the submarines tied up to the tender. The other boats are (left to right) *Rasher*, *Bowfin*, *Bluefish* and *Narwhal* seen over the bow of *Crevalle*.

the approaches to Fremantle. It was a good idea, but the elements were against them as hurricane-force winds battered the submarine for three days and, after many seasick crew members, the patrol was terminated at Fremantle on 15 March 1944.

Her fourth patrol commenced on 13 April when she headed for the Sulu Sea to operate off the coast of Mindanao. She intercepted a convoy of four ships on 26 April and gave the deep six to the 806-ton passenger-cargo *Tokiwa Maru* in a night surface attack using the submarine's radar and claimed damage to a smaller craft estimated at 500 tons. The following morning she made three hits on a freighter of approximately 4,500 tons. *Bonefish* was then ordered to check the Tawi Tawi area and while heading south Hogan was able to damage the 8,811-ton freighter *Aobasan Maru* off Zamboanga on 7 May. On the 14th, just south of the Sibutu Passage, she attacked a convoy of three tankers escorted by three destroyers, damaging a tanker estimated at 10,000 tons and putting paid to the career of

The IJN *Inadzuma* was sunk by *Bonefish* off Tawi Tawi on 14 May 1944.

Imperial Japanese Navy's destroyer *Inadzuma*. The patrol ended as she tied up at Fremantle on 24 May 1944.

Bonefish received a new skipper with Lt-Cmdr Lawrence L. Edge taking command while she was undergoing a refit. It was 25 June before she put to sea again and it was 5 July when the first engagement of the trip destroyed a schooner by gunfire. Her gun crew were again on target on the 7th when they sank the 207-ton cargo boat *Ryuei Maru* and on the following day the 60-ton *Moji Maru* went to the bottom. A 100-ton sampan was their victim on the 10th. Early in the morning of 30 July, Edge put four torpedoes into the 10,026-ton tanker *Kokuyo Maru* which sank quickly and on 3 August damaged another with one torpedo, but its fate is not known. Edge guided *Bonefish* into Fremantle on 13 August 1944.

She left Fremantle on her sixth war patrol and after calling at Darwin on 12 September she proceeded to her patrol area west of Luzon. *Bonefish* was part of a group which consisted of the USS *Flasher* (SS-249) and the USS *Lapon* (SS-260) and they were most successful with *Bonefish* herself sinking the 2,068-ton tanker *Anjo Maru* on 28 September. She attacked a small convoy on 10 October claiming hits on two freighters, each estimated at 4,000 tons, but some aggressive depth-charging forced her to stay deep and the damage could not be confirmed. Four days later she sank the 2,546-ton freighter *Fushimi Maru* with one torpedo hit. The two-man crew of a Navy SBD dive-bomber were rescued on the 18th after spending a few days drifting in their rubber boat. The flyers were safely delivered to Pearl Harbor on 8 November 1944 before she proceeded to San Francisco for a badly needed overhaul.

It was five months before *Bonefish* got back into the war as she did not begin her seventh patrol until 6 April 1945. She left Guam heading for the East China Sea and lower Tsushima Straits, but hunting was poor and her only catch was two Japanese flyers who were floating in the middle of a large patch of oil with only their life-jackets to support them. The submarine arrived back at Guam on 7 May 1945 and in the following days the crew celebrated the Victory in Europe announcement.

Anxious to get the war in the Pacific over with too, *Bonefish* departed for her eighth patrol on 28 May. With eight other submarines she was assigned to enter the Sea of Japan where no US submarine had been since the loss of the USS *Wahoo* in October 1943. New technology in the shape of FM sonar was introduced and with this equipment the minefields laid there were no longer a

Looking tired, *Bonefish* arrives at Pearl Harbor on 8 November 1944 before going on to San Francisco for an overhaul.

threat. Codenamed 'Hell Cats' all of the submarines successfully negotiated the various minefields and entered the Sea of Japan. Edge was soon on target when he sank the 6,892-ton *Oshikayama Maru* on 13 June. Part of the group, 'Pierce's Pole Cats', named after Cmdr George E. Pierce in the USS *Tunny* (SS-282), Edge in *Bonefish* requested a rendezvous with the pack leader and at the meeting on the 18th he asked if he could take his boat into Toyama Bay as target prospects looked good. *Bonefish* was credited with the sinking of the 5,485-ton freighter *Kozan Maru* on 19 June, but then she appears to have been detected and sunk by the Japanese anti-submarine forces. Post-war records show that a concentrated attack by depth-charges brought a large amount of oil and debris to the surface.

The gallant *Bonefish* was gone with Lawrence Edge and his eighty-four brave crew-members sleeping forever just a few miles from the Japanese mainland.

Bonefish received a Navy Unit Commendation for her first, third, fourth, fifth and sixth war patrols and also seven battle stars.

Lawrence Edge, *Bonefish's* skipper, was lost with the boat after entering the Sea of Japan.

US *Bullhead* (SS-332)

The Electric Boat Company launched *Bullhead* at Groton on 16 July 1944 and she was commissioned on 4 December 1944 with a Cmdr Walter T. Griffith in command. Griffith came to a new construction boat after three successful patrols in the USS *Bowfin* (SS-287).

Bullhead's launching at Groton on 16 July 1944.

Bullhead departed Pearl Harbor on 21 March 1945 to patrol the South China Sea, but found few targets. Her main duty was to operate as a lifeguard, but this nearly went wrong on 8 April when a B-24 Liberator roared out of low cloud and dropped three bombs which fell about 75 yards astern. However, the underwater explosions were enough to shake up the boat quite considerably. *Bullhead* rescued three airmen before ending her patrol at Fremantle on 27 April 1945.

The second patrol commenced after a quick replenishment of supplies as Walt Griffith took *Bullhead* to the South China Sea once more. Targets were in short supply, but on 30 May her deck gun destroyed a large schooner. A gun action was thought to have sunk a cargo ship estimated at 700 tons on 18 June. It was sinking when the submarine left the scene, but this was never confirmed and

Bullhead crew members pass food to friendly Chinese aboard a junk during her first patrol in the spring of 1945.

The last known photograph of *Bullhead* as she leaves Fremantle on 30 July 1945.

neither were three more vessels gunned by *Bullhead* the following day. The patrol ended after forty-three days at sea.

Griffith left *Bullhead* to join Admiral Lockwood's staff at Comsubpac and her new skipper was Lt-Cmdr Edward R. Holt Jr.

She left Fremantle on 30 July for her third patrol. Holt's orders were to operate in the Java Sea until 5 September then proceed to Subic Bay in the Philippines. On 6 August *Bullhead* reported that she had passed through the Lombok Strait, but just north of Bali she was bombed by a Japanese aircraft. The pilot of the Mitsubishi Ki-51 'Sonia' reported that he dropped two 60-kilogram bombs, both hitting the submarine. After the boat disappeared he saw 'a great amount of gushing water and air bubbles rising in the water'.

Bullhead was the last United States submarine to be lost in World War II and it is particularly sad as the war ended just a few days later. She received two battle stars for her short war service.

Walter Griffith, *Bullhead's* first commander, takes a periscope sighting during her first war patrol.

Appendix A
US Submarine Losses During World War II
(Chronological order)

Year	Name	Number	Date	Commander	Crew Lost
1941					
	Sealion	SS-195	Dec 10	Richard G. Voge	4
1942					
	S-36	SS-141	Jan 20	John R. McKnight Jr	0
	S-26	SS-131	Jan 24	Earle C. Hawk	46
	Shark	SS-147	Feb 11 (?)	Lewis Shane Jr (L)	58
	Perch	SS-176	Mar 3	David A. Hurt	9 (POW)
	S-27	SS-132	Jun 19	Herbert L. Jukes	0
	Grunion	SS-216	Jul-Aug	Mannert L. Abele (L)	70
	S-39	SS-144	Aug 16	Francis E. Brown	0
1943					
	Argonaut	SS-166	Jan 10	John R. Pierce (L)	105
	Amberjack	SS-219	Feb 16	John A. Bole Jr (L)	74
	Grampus	SS-207	Mar 5 (?)	John R. Craig (L)	71
	Triton	SS-201	Mar 15	George K. MacKenzie Jr (L)	74
	Pickerel	SS-177	Apr 3	Augustus H. Alston Jr (L)	74
	Grenadier	SS-210	Apr 22	John A. Fitzgerald	4 (POW)
	Runner	SS-275	May-Jul	Joseph H. Bourland (L)	78
	R-12	SS-89	Jun 12	Edward E. Shelby	42
	Grayling	SS-209	Aug-Sep	Robert M. Brinker (L)	76
	Pompano	SS-181	Aug-Sep	Willis M. Thomas (L)	76
	Cisco	SS-290	Sep 28	James W. Coe (L)	76
	S-44	SS-155	Oct 7	Francis E. Brown (L)	56
	Wahoo	SS-238	Oct 11	Dudley W. Morton (L)	80
	Dorado	SS-248	Oct 12	Earle C. Schneider (L)	76
	Corvina	SS-226	Nov 16	Roderick S. Rooney (L)	82
	Sculpin	SS-191	Nov 19	Fred Connaway (L)	12 + 51(POW)
	Capelin	SS-289	Dec 9	Elliot E. Marshall (L)	78
1944					
	Scorpion	SS-278	Jan-Feb	Maximilian G. Schmidt (L)	76
	Grayback	SS-208	Feb 26	John A. Moore (L)	80
	Trout	SS-202	Feb	Albert H. Clark (L)	81
	Tullibee	SS-284	Mar 26	Charles F. Brindupke (L)	79
	Gudgeon	SS-211	Apr-May	Robert A. Bonin (L)	78
	Herring	SS-233	Jun 1	David Zabriskie Jr (L)	84
	Golet	SS-361	Jun 14	James S. Clark (L)	82
	S-28	SS-133	Jul 4	Jack G. Campbell (L)	50
	Robalo	SS-273	Jul 26	Manning M. Kimmel (L)	77 + 4 (POW)
	Flier	SS-250	Aug 13	John D. Crowley	78
	Harder	SS-257	Aug 24	Samuel D. Dealey (L)	79
	Seawolf	SS-197	Oct 3	Albert M. Bontier (L)	82 + 17 (USA)
	Darter	SS-227	Oct 24	David H. McClintock	0
	Shark II	SS-314	Oct 24	Edward N. Blakely (L)	87

Tang	SS-306	Oct 24	Richard H. O'Kane	78
Escolar	SS-294	Oct	William J. Millican (L)	82
Albacore	SS-218	Nov 7	Hugh R. Rimmer (L)	86
Growler	SS-215	Nov 8	Thomas B. Oakley (L)	85
Scamp	SS-277	Nov 11	John C. Hollingsworth (L)	83

1945

Swordfish	SS-193	Jan 12	Keats E. Montross (L)	89
Barbel	SS-316	Feb 4	Conde L. Raguet (L)	81
Kete	SS-369	Mar	Edward Ackerman (L)	87
Trigger	SS-237	Mar 28	David R. Connole (L)	89
Snook	SS-279	Apr	John F. Walling (L)	84
Lagarto	SS-371	May 3	Frank D. Latta (L)	85
Bonefish	SS-223	Jan 18	Lawrence L. Edge (L)	85
Bullhead	SS-332	Aug 6	Edward R. Holt Jr (L)	84

(L) Lost

Appendix B

Japanese Vessels sunk by Submarines later Lost in Action
Allowance by the Post-War Joint Army-Navy Assessment
Committee (JANAC)

Date	Vessel	Type	Tonnage	Submarine Commander
USS *Albacore* (SS-218)				
Dec 18 1942	*Tenryu*	Light Cruiser	3,300	Richard C. Lake
Feb 20 1943	*Oshio*	Destroyer	1,850	Richard C. Lake
Feb 20 1943	*Unknown*	Frigate	750	Richard C. Lake
Sep 4 1943	*Heijo Maru*	ex-Gunboat	2,627	Oscar E. Hagberg
Nov 25 1943	*Kenzan Maru*	Cargo	4,704	Oscar E. Hagberg
Jan 12 1944	*Choko Maru*	ex-Gunboat	2,629	James W. Blanchard
Jan 14 1944	*Sazanami*	Destroyer	1,950	James W. Blanchard
Jun 19 1944	*Taiho*	Carrier	31,000	James W. Blanchard
Sep 5 1944	*Shingetsu M*	Cargo	880	James W. Blanchard
Sep 11 1944	*Ch.165*	Sub Chaser	170	James W. Blanchard
			49,860	
USS *Amberjack* (SS-219)				
Sep 19 1942	*Shirogane M*	Pass/Cargo	3,130	John A. Bole Jr
Oct 7 1942	*Senkai Maru*	Storeship	2,101	John A. Bole Jr
			5,231	
USS *Barbel* (SS-316)				
Aug 5 1944	*Miyako Maru*	Cargo	970	Robert A. Keating
Aug 9 1944	*Yagi Maru*	Cargo	1,937	Robert A. Keating
Aug 9 1944	*Boko Maru*	Cargo	2,333	Robert A. Keating
Sep 25 1944	*Bushu Maru*	Cargo	1,223	Robert A. Keating
Nov 14 1944	*Misaki Maru*	Cargo	4,422	Robert A. Keating
Nov 14 1944	*Sugiyama M*	Cargo	4,379	Robert A. Keating
			15,264	
USS *Bonefish* (SS-223)				
Sep 27 1943	*Kashima Maru*	Transport	9,908	Thomas W. Hogan
Oct 10 1943	*Teibi Maru*	Transport	10,086	Thomas W. Hogan
Oct 10 1943	*Isuzugawa*	Cargo	4,214	Thomas W. Hogan
Nov 29 1943	*Suez Maru*	Cargo	4,645	Thomas W. Hogan
Dec 1 1943	*Nichiryo Maru*	Pass/Cargo	2,721	Thomas W. Hogan
Apr 26 1944	*Tokiwa Maru*	Pass/Cargo	806	Thomas W. Hogan
May 14 1944	*Inazuma*	Destroyer	1,950	Thomas W. Hogan
Jul 30 1944	*Kokuyo Maru*	Tanker	10,026	Lawrence L. Edge
Sep 28 1944	*Anjo Maru*	Tanker	2,068	Lawrence L. Edge
Oct 14 1944	*Fushimi Maru*	Cargo	2,546	Lawrence L. Edge
June 13 1945	*Oshikayama M*	Cargo	6,892	Lawrence L. Edge
Jun 19 1945	*Kozan Maru*	Cargo	5,485	Lawrence L. Edge
			61,347	
USS *Capelin* (SS-289)				
Nov 11 1943	*Kunitama M*	Cargo	3,127	Elliot E. Marshall
			3,127	

USS *Darter* (SS-227)

Mar 30	1944	*Fujikawa M*	Cargo	2,829	William S. Stovall
Jun 29	1944	*Tsugaru*	Minelayer	4,400	David H. McClintock
Oct 23	1944	*Atago*	Heavy Cruiser	12,000	David H. McClintock
				19,229	

USS *Flier* (SS-250)

Jun 4	1944	*Hakusan Maru*	Transport	10,380	John D. Crowley
				10,380	

USS *Grampus* (SS-207)

Mar 1	1942	*Kaijo Maru 2*	Tanker	8,632	Edward S. Hutchinson
				8,632	

USS *Grayback* (SS-208)

Mar 17	1942	*Ishikari Maru*	ex-Collier	3,291	Williard A. Saunders
Jan 2	1943	*I-18 (?)*	Submarine	2,180	Edward C. Stephan
May 11	1943	*Yodogawa M*	Cargo	6,441	Edward C. Stephan
May 17	1943	*England Maru*	Cargo	5,829	Edward C. Stephan
Oct 14	1943	*Kozui Maru*	Pass/Cargo	7,072	John A. Moore
Oct 22	1943	*Awata Maru*	ex-L Cruiser	7,398	John A. Moore
Dec 18	1943	*Gyokurei M*	Cargo	5,588	John A. Moore
Dec 19	1943	*Numakaze*	Destroyer	1,300	John A. Moore
Dec 21	1943	*Konan Maru*	Pass/Cargo	2,627	John A. Moore
Dec 21	1943	*Kashiwa M*	ex-Netlayer	515	John A. Moore
Feb 19	1944	*Taikei Maru*	Cargo	4,739	John A. Moore
Feb 19	1944	*Toshin Maru*	Cargo	1,917	John A. Moore
Feb 24	1944	*Nampo Maru*	Tanker	10,033	John A. Moore
Feb 27	1944	*Ceylon Maru*	Cargo	4,905	John A. Moore
				63,835	

USS *Grayling* (SS-209)

Apr 13	1942	*Ryujin Maru*	Cargo	6,243	Elliot Olsen
Nov 10	1942	*Unknown*	Cargo	4,000	John E. Lee
Jan 26	1943	*Ushio Maru*	Cargo	749	John E. Lee
Apr 9	1943	*Shanghai M*	Cargo	4,103	John E. Lee
Aug 27	1943	*Meizan Maru*	Cargo	5,480	Robert M. Brinker
				20,575	

USS *Grenadier* (SS-210)

May 8	1942	*Taiyo Maru*	Transport	14,457	Willis A. Lent
				14,457	

USS *Growler* (SS-215)

Jul 5	1942	*Arare*	Destroyer	1,850	Howard W. Gilmore
Aug 25	1942	*Senyo Maru*	ex-Gunboat	2,904	Howard W. Gilmore
Aug 31	1942	*Eifuku Maru*	Cargo	5,866	Howard W. Gilmore
Sep 4	1942	*Kashino*	Supply Ship	4,000	Howard W. Gilmore
Sep 7	1942	*Taika Maru*	Cargo	2,204	Howard W. Gilmore
Jan 16	1943	*Chifuku Maru*	Pass/Cargo	5,857	Howard W. Gilmore
Jun 19	1943	*Miyadono M*	Pass/Cargo	5,196	Arnold F. Schade
Jun 29	1944	*Katori Maru*	Transport	1,920	Thomas B. Oakley Jr
Sep 12	1944	*Shikinami*	Destroyer	1,950	Thomas B. Oakley Jr
Sep 12	1944	*Hirado*	Frigate	870	Thomas B. Oakley Jr
				32,617	

USS _Grunion_ (SS-216)

Jul 15	1942	_Ch.25_	Sub Chaser	300	Mannert L. Abele
Jul 15	1942	_Ch.27_	Sub Chaser	300	Mannert L. Abele
				600	

USS _Gudgeon_ (SS-211)

Jan 27	1942	_I-73_	Submarine	1,785	Elton W. Grenfell
Mar 26	1942	_Unknown_	Cargo	4,000	Elton W. Grenfell
Mar 27	1942	_Nissho Maru_	Cargo	6,526	Elton W. Grenfell
Aug 3	1942	_Naniwa Maru_	Cargo	4,853	William S. Stovall
Oct 31	1942	_Choko Maru_	Cargo	6,783	William S. Stovall
Mar 22	1943	_Meigan Maru_	Cargo	5,434	William S. Post Jr
Mar 29	1943	_Toho Maru_	Tanker	9,987	William S. Post Jr
Apr 28	1943	_Kamakura M_	Transport	17,526	William S. Post Jr
May 12	1943	_Sumatra Maru_	Cargo	5,861	William S. Post Jr
Sep 28	1943	_Taian Maru_	Cargo	3,158	William S. Post Jr
Nov 23	1943	_Nekka Maru_	Transport	6,783	William S. Post Jr
Nov 23	1943	_Wakamiya_	Frigate	870	William S. Post Jr
				73,566	

USS _Harder_ (SS-257)

Jun 23	1943	_Sagara Maru_	ex-Seaplane Tdr	7,189	Samuel D. Dealey
Sep 9	1943	_Koyo Maru_	Cargo	3,010	Samuel D. Dealey
Sep 11	1943	_Yoko Maru_	Cargo	1,050	Samuel D. Dealey
Sep 19	1943	_Kachisan Maru_	Cargo	814	Samuel D. Dealey
Sep 23	1943	_Kowa Maru_	Cargo	4,520	Samuel D. Dealey
Sep 23	1943	_Daishin Maru_	Tanker	5,957	Samuel D. Dealey
Nov 19	1943	_Udo Maru_	Cargo	3,936	Samuel D. Dealey
Nov 19	1943	_Hokko Maru_	Cargo	5,385	Samuel D. Dealey
Nov 20	1943	_Nikko Maru_	Cargo	5,949	Samuel D. Dealey
Apr 13	1944	_Ikazuchi_	Destroyer	2,090	Samuel D. Dealey
Apr 17	1944	_Matsue Maru_	Cargo	7,061	Samuel D. Dealey
Jun 6	1944	_Minatsuki_	Destroyer	1,500	Samuel D. Dealey
Jun 7	1944	_Hayanami_	Destroyer	2,520	Samuel D. Dealey
Jun 9	1944	_Tanikaze_	Destroyer	2,033	Samuel D. Dealey
Aug 22	1944	_Matsuwa_	Frigate	870	Samuel D. Dealey
Aug 22	1944	_Hiburi_	Frigate	940	Samuel D. Dealey
				54,824	

USS _Herring_ (SS-233)

Dec 14	1943	_Hakozaki Maru_	Pass/Cargo	3,948	Raymond W. Johnson
Jan 1	1944	_Nagoya Maru_	Trans-A/c Ferry	6,071	Raymond W. Johnson
May 31	1944	_Ishigaki_	Frigate	860	David Zabriskie Jr
May 31		_Hokuyo Maru_	Cargo	1,590	David Zabriskie Jr
Jun 1	1944	_Iwaki Maru_	Transport	3,124	David Zabriskie Jr
Jun 1	1944	_Hiburi Maru_	Cargo	4,366	David Zabriskie Jr
				19,959	

USS _Herring_ (SS-233) — UK based

Nov 5	1942	_Ville de Havre_	Cargo	5,083	Raymond W. Johnson
Mar 21	1943	_U-163_	Submarine	1,153	Raymond W. Johnson
				6,236	

USS *Kete* (SS-369)

Mar 10 1945	*Keizan Maru*	Cargo	2,116	Edward Ackerman
Mar 10 1945	*Sanka Maru*	Cargo	2,945	Edward Ackerman
Mar 10 1945	*Dokan Maru*	Cargo	2,270	Edward Ackerman
			6,881	

USS *Lagarto* (SS-371)

Feb 24 1945	*Tatsumomo M*	Cargo	880	Frank D. Latta
Feb 24 1945	*I-371*	Submarine	1,440	Frank D. Latta
			2,320	

USS *Pickerel* (SS-177)

Jan 10 1942	*Kanko Maru*	Armed Cargo	2,929	Barton E. Bacon Jr
Feb 15 1943	*Tateyama M*	Auxiliary	1,990	Augustus H. Alston Jr
Apr 3 1943	*Ch.13*	Sub Chaser	440	Augustus H. Alston Jr
Apr 7 1943	*Fukuei Maru*	Cargo	1,113	Augustus H. Alston Jr
			6,472	

USS *Pompano* (SS-181)

May 25 1942	*Tokyo Maru*	Tanker	902	Lewis S. Parks
May 30 1942	*Atsuta Maru*	Transport	7,983	Lewis S. Parks
Aug 12 1942	*Unknown*	Cargo	4,000	Willis M. Thomas
Sep 3 1943	*Akama Maru*	Transport	5,600	Willis M. Thomas
Sep 25 1943	*Taiko Maru*	Auxiliary	2,958	Willis M. Thomas
			21,443	

USS *Runner* (SS-275)

Jun 11 1943	*Seinan Maru*	Cargo	1,338	Joseph H. Bourland
Jun 26 1943	*Shinryu Maru*	Cargo	4,935	Joseph H. Bourland
			6,273	

USS *S-28* (SS-133)

Sep 20 1943	*Katsura M 2*	ex-Gunboat	1,368	Vincent A. Sisler Jr
			1,368	

USS *S-39* (SS-144)

Mar 4 1942	*Erimo*	Tanker	6,500	James W. Coe
			6,500	

USS *S-44* (SS-155)

May 12 1942	*Shoei Maru*	Cargo	5,644	John R. Moore
Jun 21 1942	*Keijo Maru*	ex-Gunboat	2,626	John R. Moore
Aug 10 1942	*Kako*	Heavy Cruiser	8,800	John R. Moore
			17,070	

USS *Scamp* (SS-277)

May 29 1943	*Kamikawa M*	Cvtd Sea'p Tdr	6,853	Walter G. Ebert
Jul 27 1943	*I-168*	Submarine	1,400	Walter G. Ebert
Sep 19 1943	*Kansai Maru*	Cargo	8,614	Walter G. Ebert
Nov 10 1943	*Tokyo Maru*	Pass/Cargo	6,481	Walter G. Ebert
Jan 14 1944	*Nippon Maru*	Tanker	9,974	Walter G. Ebert
			33,322	

USS *Scorpion* (SS-278)

Apr 20	1943	*Meiji M 1*	Cvtd Gunboat	1,934	William N. Wylie
Apr 27	1943	*Yuzan Maru*	Cargo	7,500	William N. Wylie
Jul 3	1943	*Anzan Maru*	Cargo	3,890	William N. Wylie
Jul 3	1943	*Kokuryu M*	Pass/Cargo	6,112	William N. Wylie
				19,436	

USS *Sculpin* (SS-191)

Oct 7	1942	*Naminoue M*	Transport	4,731	Lucius H. Chappell
Oct 14	1942	*Sumiyoshi M*	Tanker	1,921	Lucius H. Chappell
Aug 9	1943	*Sekko Maru*	Cargo	3,183	Lucius H. Chappell
				9,835	

USS *Seawolf* (SS-197)

Jun 15	1942	*Nampo Maru*	ex-Gunboat	1,206	Frederick B. Warder
Aug 14	1942	*Hachigen M*	Pass/Cargo	3,113	Frederick B. Warder
Aug 25	1942	*Showa Maru*	Cargo	1,349	Frederick B. Warder
Nov 2	1942	*Gifu Maru*	Cargo	2,933	Frederick B. Warder
Nov 3	1942	*Sagami Maru*	Transport	7,189	Frederick B. Warder
Nov 8	1942	*Keiko Maru*	ex-Gunboat	2,929	Frederick B. Warder
Apr 15	1943	*Kaihei Maru*	Cargo	4,575	Royce L. Gross
Apr 23	1943	*PB No.39*	Patrol Boat	820	Royce L. Gross
Jun 20	1943	*Shojin Maru*	Cargo	4,739	Royce L. Gross
Aug 31	1943	*Shoto Maru*	Cargo	5,253	Royce L. Gross
Aug 31	1943	*Kokko Maru*	Cargo	5,486	Royce L. Gross
Sep 1	1943	*Fusei Maru*	Pass/Cargo	2,256	Royce L. Gross
Oct 29	1943	*Wuhu Maru*	Cargo	3,222	Royce L. Gross
Nov 4	1943	*Kaifuku M*	Pass/Cargo	3,177	Royce L. Gross
Jan 10	1944	*Asuka Maru*	Cargo	7,523	Royce L. Gross
Jan 10	1944	*Getsuyo M*	Cargo	6,440	Royce L. Gross
Jan 11	1944	*Yahiko Maru*	Cargo	5,747	Royce L. Gross
Jan 14	1944	*Yamatsuru M*	Cargo	3,651	Royce L. Gross
				71,608	

USS *Shark II* (SS-314)

Jun 2	1944	*Chiyo Maru*	Cargo	4,700	Edward N. Blakely
Jun 4	1944	*Katsukawa M*	Cargo	6,886	Edward N. Blakely
Jun 5	1944	*Takaoka Maru*	Cargo	7,006	Edward N. Blakely
Jun 5	1944	*Tamahime M*	Cargo	3,080	Edward N. Blakely
				21,672	

USS *Snook* (SS-279)

May 5	1943	*Kinko Maru*	Cargo	1,268	Charles O. Triebel
May 5	1943	*Daifuku Maru*	Cargo	3,194	Charles O. Triebel
May 7	1943	*Tosei Maru*	Cargo	4,363	Charles O. Triebel
Jul 4	1943	*Liverpool M*	Cargo	5,865	Charles O. Triebel
Jul 4	1943	*Koki Maru*	Cargo	5,290	Charles O. Triebel
Sep 13	1943	*Yamato Maru*	Transport	9,655	Charles O. Triebel
Sep 22	1943	*Katsurahama M*	Cargo	715	Charles O. Triebel
Nov 29	1943	*Yamafuku M*	Pass/Cargo	4,928	Charles O. Triebel
Nov 29	1943	*Shiganoura M*	Cargo	3,512	Charles O. Triebel
Jan 23	1944	*Magane Maru*	Cvtd Gunboat	3,120	Charles O. Triebel
Feb 8	1944	*Lima Maru*	Cargo	6,989	Charles O. Triebel
Feb 14	1944	*Nittoku M*	Cargo	3,591	Charles O. Triebel
Feb 15	1944	*Hoshi M 2*	Cargo	875	Charles O. Triebel

Feb 23	1944	*Koyo Maru*	Pass/Cargo	5,471	Charles O. Triebel
Oct 23	1944	*Kikusui Maru*	Tanker	3,887	George H. Browne
Oct 24	1944	*Arisan Maru*	Cargo	6,886	George H. Browne
Oct 24	1944	*Shinsei M 1*	Cargo	5,863	George H. Browne
				75,472	

USS *Swordfish* (SS-193)

Dec 16	1941	*Atsutasan Maru*	Cargo	8,663	Chester C. Smith
Jan 24	1942	*Myoken Maru*	Cargo	4,124	Chester C. Smith
Jun 12	1942	*Burma Maru*	Cargo	4,585	Chester C. Smith
Jan 19	1943	*Myoho Maru*	Cargo	4,122	Jack H. Lewis
Aug 22	1943	*Nishiyama M*	Cargo	3,016	Frank M. Parker
Sep 5	1943	*Tenkai Maru*	Cargo	3,203	Frank M. Parker
Jan 14	1944	*Yamakuni M*	Pass/Cargo	6,925	Karl G. Hensel
Jan 16	1944	*Delhi Maru*	Cvtd Gunboat	2,182	Karl G. Hensel
Jan 27	1944	*Kasagi Maru*	Cvtd Salvage	3,140	Karl G. Hensel
Jun 9	1944	*Matsukaze*	Destroyer	1,270	Keats E. Montross
Jun 15	1944	*Kanseishi M*	Cargo	4,804	Keats E. Montross
				46,034	

Note: *Tatsufuku Maru* originally credited to *Swordfish* for 29 May 1942 passed to USS *Seal* (SS-183).

USS *Tang* (SS-306)

Feb 17	1944	*Gyoten Maru*	Cargo	6,854	Richard H. O'Kane
Feb 22	1944	*Fukuyama M*	Pass/Cargo	3,581	Richard H. O'Kane
Feb 23	1944	*Yamashimo M*	Cargo	6,777	Richard H. O'Kane
Feb 24	1944	*Echizen Maru*	Cargo	2,424	Richard H. O'Kane
Feb 25	1944	*Choko Maru**	Tanker	1,790	Richard H. O'Kane
Jun 24	1944	*Tamahoko M*	Pass/Cargo	6,780	Richard H. O'Kane
Jun 24	1944	*Tainan Maru*	Cargo	3,175	Richard H. O'Kane
Jun 24	1944	*Nasusan M*	Pass/Cargo	4,399	Richard H. O'Kane
Jun 24	1944	*Kennichi M*	Cargo	1,937	Richard H. O'Kane
Jun 30	1944	*Nikkin Maru*	Cargo	5,705	Richard H. O'Kane
Jul 1	1944	*Takatori M*	Tanker	878	Richard H. O'Kane
Jul 1	1944	*Taiun M 2*	Cargo	998	Richard H. O'Kane
Jul 4	1944	*Asukazan*	Cargo	6,886	Richard H. O'Kane
Jul 4	1944	*Yamaoka Maru*	Cargo	6,932	Richard H. O'Kane
Jul 6	1944	*Dori Maru*	Cargo	1,469	Richard H. O'Kane
Aug 11	1944	*Roko Maru*	Cargo	3,328	Richard H. O'Kane
Aug 23	1944	*Tsukushi M*	Transport	8,135	Richard H. O'Kane
Oct 10	1944	*Joshu Go*	Cargo	1,658	Richard H. O'Kane
Oct 11	1944	*Oita Maru*	Cargo	711	Richard H. O'Kane
Oct 23	1944	*Toun Maru*	Cargo	1,915	Richard H. O'Kane
Oct 23	1944	*Wakatake M*	Cargo	1,920	Richard H. O'Kane
Oct 23	1944	*Tatsuju Maru*	Cargo	1,944	Richard H. O'Kane
Oct 24	1944	*Matsumoto M*	Tanker	7,024	Richard H. O'Kane
Oct 24	1944	*Kogen Maru*	Tanker	6,600	Richard H. O'Kane
				93,820	

* It is believed that the *Choko Maru* was a large tanker and that a JANAC or Japanese clerical error omitted a figure zero from the end of the vessel's tonnage.

USS *Trigger* (SS-237)

Oct 17	1942	*Holland Maru*	Transport	5,869	Roy S. Benson
Dec 22	1942	*Teifuku Maru*	Cargo	5,198	Roy S. Benson
Jan 10	1943	*Okikaze*	Destroyer	1,215	Roy S. Benson

Mar 15 1943	*Momoha Maru*	Transport	3,103	Roy S. Benson
Jun 1 1943	*Noborikawa M*	Cargo	2,182	Roy S. Benson
Sep 18 1943	*Yowa Maru*	Cargo	6,435	Robert E. Dornin
Sep 21 1943	*Shiriya**	Tanker	6,500	Robert E. Dornin
Sep 21 1943	*Shoyo Maru*	Tanker	7,498	Robert E. Dornin
Sep 21 1943	*Argun Maru*	Cargo	6,662	Robert E. Dornin
Nov 2 1943	*Delagoa M*	Transport	7,148	Robert E. Dornin
Nov 2 1943	*Yawata Maru*	Cargo	1,852	Robert E. Dornin
Nov 13 1943	*Nachisan M*	Transport	4,443	Robert E. Dornin
Nov 21 1943	*Eizan Maru*	Cargo	1,681	Robert E. Dornin
Jan 31 1944	*Yasukuni M*	Cvtd Sub Tdr	11,933	Robert E. Dornin
Jan 31 1944	*Nasami***	Coast M'layer	443	Robert E. Dornin
Apr 27 1944	*Miike Maru*	Pass/Cargo	11,738	Frederick. J. Harlfinger II
Mar 18 1945	*Tsukushi M 3*	Cargo	1,012	David R. Connole
Mar 27 1945	*Odate*	Repair Ship	1,564	David R. Connole
			86,551	

* Japanese sources quote *Shiriya* as 14,050 tons, but for unknown reason JANAC only allowed 6,500 tons!

** JANAC credited *Trigger* with the *Nasami*, but Japanese report this vessel sunk at Rabaul 1 April 1944 after air attack!

USS Triton (SS-201)

Feb 17 1942	*Shinyo M 5*	Cargo	1,498	Willis A. Lent
Feb 21 1942	*Shokyo Maru*	Cargo	4,486	Willis A. Lent
Apr 23 1942	*Unknown*	Trawler	1,000	Charles C. Kirkpatrick
May 1 1942	*Calcutta M*	Pass/Cargo	5,338	Charles C. Kirkpatrick
May 6 1942	*Taiei Maru*	Cargo	2,208	Charles C. Kirkpatrick
May 6 1942	*Taigen Maru*	Pass/Cargo	5,665	Charles C. Kirkpatrick
May 17 1942	*I-64 (I-164)*	Submarine	1,635	Charles C. Kirkpatrick
Jul 4 1942	*Nenohi*	Destroyer	1,600	Charles C. Kirkpatrick
Dec 24 1942	*Amakasu M 1*	Water Carrier	1,913	Charles C. Kirkpatrick
Dec 28 1942	*Omi Maru*	Pass/Cargo	3,394	Charles C. Kirkpatrick
Mar 6 1943	*Kiriha Maru*	Cargo	3,057	George K. MacKenzie Jr
			31,794	

USS Trout (SS-202)

Feb 10 1942	*Chuwa Maru*	Cargo	2,719	Frank W. Fenno Jr
May 2 1942	*Uzan Maru*	Cargo	5,014	Frank W. Fenno Jr
May 4 1942	*Kongosan Maru*	Cvtd Gunboat	2,119	Frank W. Fenno Jr
Sep 21 1942	*Koei Maru*	Cvtd Net Tdr	863	Lawson P. Ramage
Jan 21 1943	*Unknown*	Cargo	2,984	Lawson P. Ramage
Feb 14 1943	*Hirotama M*	Cvtd Gunboat	1,911	Lawson P. Ramage
Jun 15 1943	*Sanraku Maru*	Tanker	3,000	Albert H. Clark
Jul 2 1943	*Isuzu Maru*	Cargo	2,866	Albert H. Clark
Sep 9 1943	*I-182**	Submarine	1,630	Albert H. Clark
Sep 23 1943	*Ryotoku Maru*	Cargo	3,483	Albert H. Clark
Sep 23 1943	*Yamashiro M*	Pass/Cargo	3,427	Albert H. Clark
Feb 29 1944	*Sakito Maru*	Pass/Cargo	7,126	Albert H. Clark
			37,142	

* JANAC credited *Trout* with the destruction of the Japanese Submarine *I-182*, but Japanese records show no loss that day. The *I-182* was most certainly sunk by the USS *Wadsworth* (DD-516) on 1 September 1943.

USS Tullibee (SS-284)

Aug 22 1943	*Kaisho Maru*	Pass/Cargo	4,164	Charles F. Brindupke

Oct 15	1943	*Chicago Maru*	Pass/Cargo	5,866	Charles F. Brindupke
Jan 31	1944	*Hiro Maru*	Net Tender	549	Charles F. Brindupke
				10,579	

USS *Wahoo* (SS-238)

Dec 10	1942	*Kamoi Maru*	Cargo	5,355	Marvin G. Kennedy
Jan 26	1943	*Unknown*	Cargo	4,000	Dudley W. Morton
Jan 26	1943	*Buyo Maru*	Transport	5,447	Dudley W. Morton
Jan 26	1943	*Fukuei M 2*	Cargo	1,901	Dudley M. Morton
Mar 19	1943	*Zogen Maru*	Cargo	1,428	Dudley W. Morton
Mar 19	1943	*Kowa Maru*	Transport	3,217	Dudley W. Morton
Mar 21	1943	*Nittsu Maru*	Cargo	2,183	Dudley W. Morton
Mar 21	1943	*Hozan Maru*	Cargo	2,260	Dudley W. Morton
Mar 23	1943	*Unknown*	Cargo	2,427	Dudley W. Morton
Mar 25	1943	*Takaosan M*	Cargo	2,076	Dudley W. Morton
Mar 25	1943	*Satsuki M*	Cargo	830	Dudley W. Morton
Mar 25	1943	*Unknown*	Cargo	2,556	Dudley W. Morton
Mar 29	1943	*Yamabato M*	Cargo	2,556	Dudley W. Morton
May 7	1943	*Tamon M 5*	Pass/Cargo	5,260	Dudley W. Morton
May 9	1943	*Takao Maru*	Cargo	3,204	Dudley W. Morton
May 9	1943	*Jinmu Maru*	Cargo	1,912	Dudley W. Morton
Sep 29	1943	*Masaki M 2*	Cargo	1,238	Dudley W. Morton
Oct 5	1943	*Konron Maru*	Transport	7,903	Dudley W. Morton
Oct 6	1943	*Unknown*	Pass/Cargo	1,283	Dudley W. Morton
Oct 9	1943	*Kanko Maru*	Cargo	2,995	Dudley W. Morton
				60,031	

Note: In the years since the Joint Army-Navy Assessment Committee's findings on individual submarine successes many facts have emerged on names, dates, tonnages and other details. The additions have been added to the above listing for completion, but the allowances are as original. Because of the nature of submarine warfare it was difficult to finally evaluate all of the attacks with the ultimate sinking or otherwise, but there is no doubt that the JANAC reached a number of strange conclusions.

Appendix C
Presidential Unit Citations awarded to Submarines lost in action

USS *Albacore*	(SS-218)	Patrols 2, 3, 7, 8
USS *Gudgeon*	(SS-211)	Patrols 1, 2, 3, 4, 5, 6, 7, 8
USS *Harder*	(SS-257)	Patrols 1, 2, 3, 4, 5
USS *Tang*	(SS-306)	Patrols 1, 2, 3, 4, 5
USS *Trigger*	(SS-237)	Patrols 5, 6, 7
USS *Trout*	(SS-202)	Patrols 2, 3, 5
USS *Wahoo*	(SS-238)	Patrols 3

Presidential Unit Citations awarded to Submarines lost in action

USS *Bonefish*	(SS-223)	Patrols 1, 3, 4, 5, 6
USS *Darter*	(SS-227)	Patrols 4
USS *Grayback*	(SS-208)	Patrols 7, 8, 9, 10
USS *Growler*	(SS-215)	Patrols 1, 2, 4, 10
USS *Seawolf*	(SS-197)	Patrols 4, 7, 10, 12
USS *Swordfish*	(SS-193)	Patrols 1, 2, 4
USS *Trigger*	(SS-237)	Patrols 9

Appendix D
United States Submarine Specifications

FLEET BOATS

Argonaut Class

Displacement (tons)	:	2,878 (surface), 4,045 (submerged)
Dimensions (feet)	:	360 (WL), 381 (OA) x 33.8 x 16
Machinery	:	two diesels plus electric motors, 3,175 bhp/2,200 shp
Performance (knots)	:	13.7 (surface), 7.5 (submerged)
Armament	:	four 21-inch TT (bow)
		two 6-inch and two 30-calibre guns
Crew	:	89
Diving depth (feet)	:	300
War loss	:	*Argonaut* (SS-166/APS-1 ex V-4)

Shark Class

Displacement (tons)	:	1,315 (surface), 1,968 (submerged)
Dimensions (feet)	:	290 (WL), 298 (OA) x 25.1 x 15.1
Machinery	:	two-shaft diesel-electrics plus electric motors, 4,300 bhp/2,085 shp
Performance (knots)	:	19.5 (surface), 8 (submerged)
Armament	:	six 21-inch TT (4 bow, 2 stern)
		one 3-inch/50 gun, two 50-calibre guns, four 30-calibre guns
Crew	:	54
Diving depth (feet)	:	250
War loss	:	*Shark* (SS-174 ex P-3)

Perch Class

Displacement (tons)	:	1,330 (surface), 1,997 (submerged)
Dimensions (feet)	:	292.6 (WL), 300.6 (OA) x 25.2 x 15.2
Machinery	:	two-shaft diesel-electrics plus electric motors, 4,300 bhp/2,366 shp
Performance (knots)	:	19.25 (surface), 8 (submerged)
Armament	:	six 21-inch TT (4 bow, 2 stern)
		one 3-inch/50 gun, two 50-calibre guns, four 30-calibre guns
Crew	:	54
Diving depth (feet)	:	250
War loss	:	*Perch* (SS-176 ex P-5), *Pickerel* (SS-177 ex P-6), *Pompano* (SS-181 ex P-10)

Sargo Class

Displacement (tons)	:	1,450 (surface), 2,198 (submerged)
Dimensions (feet)	:	302.6 (WL), 310.6 (OA) x 26.10 x 16.8
Machinery	:	two-shaft diesel-electrics plus electric motors, 5,500 bhp/2,740 shp
Performance (knots)	:	20 (surface), 8.75 (submerged)
Armament	:	eight 21-inch TT (4 bow, 2 stern)
		one 3-inch/50 gun, two 50-calibre guns, two 30-calibre guns
Crew	:	70
Diving depth (feet)	:	250

| War loss | : | *Sculpin* (SS-191 ex S-10), *Swordfish* (SS-193), *Sealion* (SS-195), *Seawolf* (SS-197) |

Tambor Class

Displacement (tons)	:	1,475 (surface), 2,370 (submerged)
Dimensions (feet)	:	302.6 (WL), 307.2 (OA) x 27.3 x 15
Machinery	:	two-shaft diesel-electrics plus electric motors, 5,400 bhp/2,740 shp
Performance (knots)	:	20 (surface), 8.75 (submerged)
Armament	:	ten 21-inch TT (6 bow, 4 stern) one 3-inch/50 gun, two 50-calibre guns
Crew	:	70
Diving depth (feet)	:	250
War loss	:	*Triton* (SS-201), *Trout* (SS-202), *Grampus* (SS-207), *Grayback* (SS-208), *Grayling* (SS-209), *Grenadier* (SS-210), *Gudgeon* (SS-211)

Gato and Balao Classes

Displacement (tons)	:	1,526 (surface), Gato 2,410 and Balao 2,415 (submerged)
Dimensions (feet)	:	311.9 (WL) (OA) x 27.3 x 15.3
Machinery	:	two-shaft diesel-electrics plus electric motors, 5,400 bhp/2,740 shp
Performance (knots)	:	20.25 (surface), 8.75 (submerged)
Armament	:	ten 21-inch TT (6 bow, 4 stern) one 3-inch/50 gun, two 50-calibre guns, two 30-calibre guns
Crew	:	80-85
Diving depth (feet)	:	300
War loss	:	**Gato**: *Growler* (SS-215), *Grunion* (SS-216), *Albacore* (SS-218), *Amberjack* (SS-219), *Bonefish* (SS-223), *Corvina* (SS-226), *Darter* (SS-227), *Herring* (SS-233), *Trigger* (SS-237), *Wahoo* (SS-238), *Dorado* (SS-248), *Flier* (SS-250), *Harder* (SS-257), *Robalo* (SS-273), *Runner* (SS-275), *Scamp* (SS-277), *Scorpion* (SS-278), *Snook* (SS-279), *Tullibee* (SS-284). **Balao**: *Capelin* (SS-289), *Cisco* (SS-290), *Escolar* (SS-294), *Tang* (SS-306), *Shark II* (SS-314), *Barbel* (SS-316), *Bullhead* (SS-332), *Golet* (SS-361), *Kete* (SS-369), *Lagarto* (SS-371)

OLDER TYPES

R Class

Displacement (tons)	:	569 (surface), 680 (submerged)
Dimensions (feet)	:	179 (WL), 186 (OA) x 18 x 14.6
Machinery	:	two shafts: diesels plus electric motors, 1,200 bhp/934 shp
Performance (knots)	:	13.5 (surface), 10.5 (submerged)
Armament	:	four 21-inch TT, one 3-inch/50 gun

Crew	:	33
Diving depth (feet)	:	200
War loss	:	*R-12* (SS-89)

S Class

Displacement (tons)	:	854 (surface), 1,062 (submerged)
Dimensions (feet)	:	211 (WL), 219.3 (OA) x 20.9 x 16
Machinery	:	two shafts: diesel engines plus electric motors, 1,200 bhp/1,500 shp
Performance (knots)	:	14.5 (surface), 11 (submerged)
Armament	:	four 21-inch TT, one 4-inch/50 gun
Crew	:	42
Diving depth (feet)	:	200
War loss	:	*S-26* (SS-131), *S-27* (SS-132), *S-28* (SS-133), *S-36* (SS-141), *S-39* (SS-144), *S-44* (SS-155)

Note: The above specifications are origin basic figures. Wartime changes to all classes were many and frequent with crew numbers, armament, equipment, etc, varying from boat to boat.

Besides the disastrous performance of the torpedoes a number of boats experienced engine problems and many completed war patrols with one or two engines inoperative. The engines in question were originally fitted to submarines in the *SS-253* to *SS-264* batch and were Hoover, Owens, Rentschler (HOR) diesels. The unreliable engines had to be replaced and this operation took many submarines out of the firing line for two months or more. One skipper declared that the HOR engines have saved Japan "about 30 to 40 vessels".

Appendix E
Submarine Memorials in the United States

Tributes to the memory of United States submariners lost during World War Two feature in Museums and Memorials throughout the country. Besides the fine work in preserving submarines themselves, many veteran associations have contributed greatly to honouring the memory of their colleagues and none more so than The US Submarine Veterans of World War Two.

The main memorials to lost submariners can be found at:

The USS *Bowfin* Submarine Museum and Park, Arizona Drive, Honolulu, Hawaii. The Waterfront Memorial was officially opened on 11 May 1992 in a ceremony attended by many veterans of the Submarine Force and with each of the 52 lost boats being individually honoured it is a fine tribute to their sacrifice.

The Submarine Base at Pearl Harbor, Hawaii, also has a fine memorial listing all the lost boats and their crew members. However, because of security at the base, this can only be seen by appointment.

The Admiral Nimitz Center at Fredricksburg, Texas, has a number of submarine exhibits and, in tribute to a gallant Texan, it has a plaque honouring Sam Dealey and his immortal *Harder*.

Another memorial in Texas honours the great *Seawolf*, its crew and the 17 army personnel lost in her when she was mistakenly sunk by friendly forces. It is located with the battleship *Texas* at La Porte, Houston.

Battleship Park in Mobile, Alabama, has the battle wagon of the same name, the submarine *Drum* in near original condition and an excellent representative of a World War Two boat. Additionally a number of memorials include David Zabriskie's *Herring* and a fine tablet to Howard W. Gilmore of the *Growler*.

The *Batfish* is another submarine on view and can be found in Muskogee, Oklahoma. A torpedo has been incorporated into a memorial to the *Shark* lost in 1942.

Other torpedoes are in various monuments, with *Wahoo* in the town of Wahoo, Nebraska, *Swordfish* at St Paul, Minnesota, and the *Trout* located near Falmouth in Massachusetts are all excellent tributes to lost submariners.

Naval establishments bear the names of many famous submariners in the buildings, with a fine example being Morton Hall in honour of the brilliant 'Mush' Morton whose *Wahoo* deprived the Japanese merchant marine of over 19 vessels whilst under his command.

All of these memorials help to preserve the history of the Silent Service to inspire future generations to pay reverence to all who earned their place in history.

Appendix F
State Assignments for Lost Submarines
(To Honour and Perpetuate the Memory
of those Submariners who lost their lives)

USS *Sealion*	Georgia	USS *Grayback*	Indiana
USS *S-36*	Iowa	USS *Trout*	Massachusetts
USS *S-26*	Alaska	USS *Tullibee*	Mississippi
USS *Shark*	Oklahoma	USS *Gudgeon*	New Jersey
USS *Perch*	Arizona	USS *Herring*	Alabama
USS *S-27*	Idaho	USS *Golet*	Louisiana
USS *Grunion*	Ohio	USS *S-28*	North Carolina
USS *S-39*	Maryland	USS *Robalo*	North Dakota
USS *Argonaut*	California	USS *Flier*	Vermont
USS *Amberjack*	South Carolina	USS *Harder*	Utah
USS *Grampus*	California	USS *Seawolf*	Texas
USS *Triton*	Connecticut	USS *Darter*	Tennessee
USS *Pickerel*	Montana	USS *Shark II*	Virginia
USS *Grenadier*	New York (West)	USS *Tang*	Florida
USS *Runner*	New York (East)	USS *Escolar*	Michigan
USS *R-12*	Rhode Island	USS *Albacore*	Oregon
USS *Grayling*	Colorado	USS *Growler*	Hawaii
USS *Pompano*	Kentucky	USS *Scamp*	Missouri
USS *Cisco*	West Virginia	USS *Swordfish*	Minnesota
USS *S-44*	Illinois	USS *Barbel*	Wyoming
USS *Wahoo*	Nebraska	USS *Kete*	Delaware
USS *Dorado*	Kansas	USS *Trigger*	Pennsylvania
USS *Corvina*	Nevada	USS *Snook*	Arkansas
USS *Sculpin*	Maine	USS *Lagarto*	Wisconsin
USS *Capelin*	New Hampshire	USS *Bonefish*	Washington
USS *Scorpion*	South Dakota	USS *Bullhead*	New Mexico

Bibliography

Sources

U.S. SUBMARINES LOSSES IN WORLD WAR II. U.S. Government, Washgton, D.C., 1949

JAPANESE NAVAL AND MERCHANT SHIPPING LOSSES – DURING W.W.II ALL CAUSES. Prepared by The Joint Army-Navy Assessment Committee. U.S. Government, Washngton, D.C., 1947

THE CAMPAIGNS OF THE PACIFIC WAR. Prepared by the Naval Analysis Division. U.S. Government, Washington, D.C., 1946

SUBMARINE WAR PATROL REPORTS, 1941–1945. U.S. Naval Historical Centre, Washington, D.C.

U.S. SUBMARINE OPERATIONS IN WORLD WAR II. Theodore Roscoe, U.S. Naval Institute, Annapolis, Maryland, 1949.

SILENT VICTORY. Clay Blair, Jr., J. B. Lippincott Co., N.Y., 1975

UNDERSEA VICTORY. Capt. W. J. Holmes, Doubleday & Company, Garden City, N.Y., 1966

U.S. SUBMARINE ATTACKS DURING WORLD WAR II. John D. Alden, U.S. Naval Institute, Annapolis, Maryland, 1989

THE FLEET SUBMARINE IN THE U.S. NAVY. J. D. Alden, U.S. Naval Institute, Annapolis, Maryland, 1979.

SUBMARINE! Edward L. Beach, William Heinemann Ltd., London, 1953

U.S.S. SEAWOLF. Frank and Horan, Putnam's Sons, New York, 1945

OVERDUE AND PRESUMED LOST – U.S.S. BULLHEAD. Martin Sheridan, Marshall Jones Company, Francestown, New Hampshire, 1947

SINK 'EM ALL. Charles A. Lockwood, E. P. Dutton & Co., Inc., New York, 1951.

WAKE OF THE WAHOO. Forest J. Sterling, Chilton Company, 1960

THE IMPERIAL JAPANESE NAVY. Watts and Gordon, MacDonald, London.

FIGHTING SHIPS OF THE IMPERIAL JAPANESE NAVY. Shizuo Fukui, KK Best Sellers, Chiyodaku, Tokyo, 1970

SUBMARINES OF THE IMPERIAL JAPANESE NAVY 1904–1945. Polmar and Carpenter, Conway Maritime Press, London, 1986

Personal Letters from Submarine Commanders, Officers and Crew Members over 30 years. Many are now members of that fine organisation U.S. SUBMARINE VETERANS OF WORLD WAR II.

Index